A Taste of Turkish Cuisine

The **Hippocrene Cookbook** library

AFRICA AND OCEANIA
The Best of Regional African Cooking
Good Food from Australia
Taste of Eritrea
Traditional South African Cookery

ASIA AND MIDDLE EAST
Afghan Food and Cookery
The Art of Persian Cooking
The Art of Turkish Cooking
The Art of Uzbek Cooking
The Best of Korean Cuisine
The Best of Regional Thai Cuisine
The Best of Taiwanese Cuisine
The Cuisine of the Caucasus Mountains
Egyptian Cooking
Flavors of Burma
Healthy South Indian Cooking
Imperial Mongolian Cooking
The Indian Spice Kitchen
Japanese Home Cooking
Sephardic Israeli Cuisine
A Taste of Syria
A Taste of Turkish Cuisine

MEDITERRANEAN
The Best of Greek Cuisine, Expanded
Edition
A Spanish Family Cookbook
Taste of Malta
Tastes of North Africa
Tastes of the Pyrenees, Classic and Modern

WESTERN EUROPE
The Art of Dutch Cooking, Expanded
Edition
The Art of Irish Cooking
A Belgian Cookbook
Cooking in the French Fashion (bilingual)
Cuisines of Portuguese Encounters
Feasting Galore Irish-Style
The Scottish-Irish Pub and Hearth
Cookbook
The Swiss Cookbook
Traditional Food from Scotland
Traditional Food from Wales
A Treasury of Italian Cuisine (bilingual)

SCANDINAVIA
The Best of Scandinavian Cooking
The Best of Finnish Cooking
The Best of Smorgasbord Cooking
Icelandic Food & Cookery
Tastes & Tales of Norway

CENTRAL EUROPE
All Along the Rhine
All Along the Danube
The Art of Hungarian Cooking
Bavarian Cooking
The Best of Austrian Cuisine
The Best of Czech Cooking
The Best of Polish Cooking
The Best of Slovak Cooking
Hungarian Cookbook
Old Warsaw Cookbook
Old Polish Traditions
Poland's Gourmet Cuisine
The Polish Country Kitchen Cookbook
Polish Heritage Cookery
Treasury of Polish Cuisine (bilingual)

EASTERN EUROPE
The Art of Lithuanian Cooking
The Best of Albanian Cooking
The Best of Croatian Cooking
The Best of Russian Cooking
The Best of Ukrainian Cuisine
Taste of Romania
Taste of Latvia
Traditional Bulgarian Cooking

AMERICAS
Argentina Cooks!
The Art of Brazilian Cookery
The Art of South American Cookery
Cooking With Cajun Women
Cooking the Caribbean Way
French Caribbean Cuisine
Mayan Cooking
Old Havana Cookbook (bilingual)
A Taste of Haiti
A Taste of Quebec

REFERENCE
International Dictionary of Gastronomy

A Taste of Turkish Cuisine

Nur İlkin
Sheilah Kaufman

HIPPOCRENE BOOKS, INC.
NEW YORK

Also by Sheilah Kaufman:
Sephardic Israeli Cuisine

Copyright © 2002 Nur İlkin and Sheilah Kaufman
Second printing, 2004.

Photographs by Maurice Asseo and Dalia Carmel.
Interior art by Gulen Tangoren.

Book and jacket design by Acme Klong Design, Inc.

For more information, address:
HIPPOCRENE BOOKS, INC.
171 Madison Avenue
New York, NY 10016

ISBN 0-7818-0948-7
Cataloging-in-Publication Data available from the Library of Congress.
Printed in the United States of America.

Nur's Dedication: To the four men in my life, my late father Ahmet Dagli who taught me to love, to care, to share, and to tolerate.

And to my dearest husband Baki İlkin and my beloved sons Murat İlkin and Mehmet Can İlkin for all the love, care, and support they've always provided.

We wish to thank Semin Cagin Zaimler, Chef Ali Tonbul, Necla Akgül, and Firdevs Demirci for their great help in making this book possible.

This book is indebted to Maurice Asseo and Dalia Carmel for their fabulous photographs of Turkey and Gulen Tangoren for her wonderful drawing.

Contents

Introduction

When I was a child, my paternal grandmother Fatma Dagli lived with us. She was a petite lady with great flair and personality from the provincial city of Gaziantep, in southeast Turkey. Gaziantep is known for its fine food, especially for its desserts and sweets. My mother worked so my grandmother did most of the cooking. She was a wonderful cook so everyone was very happy with this arrangement.

At 6 or 7, I became curious about my grandmother's cooking. I would hang out in the kitchen and watch her closely, asking many questions. Only later did I realize just how much I had learned from her. I noticed I still chop vegetables exactly as she did.

As I grew older, she gave me a more formal culinary instruction. I was her only granddaughter and she spared no effort in teaching me how to cook, including her philosophy and methods. In many ways, her cooking reflected the story of her life.

During World War I she struggled to find enough food to feed my father, her only surviving child. For the remainder of her life she was careful never to waste anything and she taught me to do the same. In her eyes it was a sin to leave food on the plate. Adversity inspired her resourcefulness and creativity, and she stressed that a good cook was someone who could make a delicious meal from whatever ingredients were available. Thanks to my grandmother I developed a real appreciation and enthusiasm for food and food preparation.

Despite my grandmother's instructions, I really did not cook until I got married. My diplomat husband, Baki, was posted to Athens on his first assignment and my culinary skills at the time consisted of family recipes and a Turkish cookbook that my father had given me before our departure. For the remainder of his life my father made it a point to give me the latest cookbooks and magazines on Turkish cuisine!

In Athens, I suddenly had to cook for my husband and myself. I began with simple dishes and progressed to more sophisticated ones. I must admit those dishes were not initially very successful, but as I practiced my skills improved. Although the food was not always terrific, Baki kindly complimented me on everything I made and encouraged my cooking efforts. Initially it couldn't have been easy for him since his mother was an excellent cook, well versed in Turkish and Arabic cuisine, and Baki was used to her delicious meals. When we returned to Turkey for our vacations she taught me a lot about cooking and shared her secrets for preparing

Baki's favorite dishes. The more I learned the more interested I became.

From Athens, we were posted to Moscow in 1974. There was very little variety of vegetables and fruits available. Since my grandmother had taught me to be creative in preparing delicious dishes with a minimum of ingredients, I began using the dried beans and vegetables my mother sent us. While there, I also learned to dry my own herbs (mint, dill, tarragon, and parsley) using my grandmother's methods (which I still do today). They all taste fresh and flavorful!

Our next assignment was London, where it was a welcome change to find an extensive variety of fresh foods. Besides continuing to develop my knowledge of international cuisine, I gave numerous Turkish cooking demonstrations at the Anglo-Turkish Society.

The ultimate test of my Turkish cooking skills came when we were transferred to Pakistan (where Baki had been appointed ambassador). Until then, we had entertained on a small scale (close groups of friends), but now we were expected to entertain much larger groups as Turkey's official representatives. Intimate dinner parties were replaced by large formal gatherings. I felt it was my responsibility to introduce our Pakistani guests to the pleasures of Turkish cuisine.

Since Baki was ambassador, I assumed that a chef would plan our official functions with a little help or guidance from me. Imagine my initial surprise when I found out that the embassy's chef was a Pakistani cook who had been hired recently and was totally unfamiliar with Turkish cuisine. I found myself back in the kitchen! We started from scratch with my family recipes for pickles, jams, and simple lemonade with mint. For the next four years, the kitchen ran under my guidance and, over time, I learned which Turkish dishes really appealed to the Pakistani palate. I then prepared menus accordingly. By the end of our stay, the Pakistani cook had become quite proficient in preparing Turkish food and I had again expanded my own knowledge of cooking.

Our next assignment was Copenhagen where we had an excellent Turkish chef who did not require my presence in the kitchen. He had a thorough knowledge and understanding of Turkish cuisine and we exchanged many recipes. Sometimes I would go to the kitchen and work with him for my own enjoyment. I even learned how to prepare a variety of delicious Danish dishes and shared some of my Turkish recipes with my new Danish friends. Interestingly enough, many of the basic ingredients of Turkish cuisine such as lentils, chickpeas, and fava beans were readily available in Danish health food stores but most people did not quite know what to do with them! Following a dinner party at the embassy, the food editor of the Danish daily *Jyllands-Posten* asked me to share my recipes with the newspaper. I was very pleased to contribute a number of recipes that I hoped gave people some insight into how to prepare those (previously) puzzling foods.

After a brief posting in the Netherlands came our posting as ambassador in Washington, D.C. The rich diversity of foods in the United States allowed me to learn much about both American cuisine and the cuisine of numerous countries and cultures, further enhancing my culinary knowledge.

Because of our travels, I began trying to integrate foreign and Turkish recipes, developing my own fusion cooking, and from elementary Turkish and international dishes I have progressed to more sophisticated recipes. The compliments that I have received have encouraged me to continue enhancing my repertoire and my greatest gift has been the enthusiasm and appreciation that my guests have offered for my food.

Cooking and cuisines are constantly changing, with many new things to learn in order to grow as a cook. I try to keep abreast of new trends from new publications on Turkish and international cuisine. It has been my privilege to be exposed to the cuisines of many countries, but Turkish cuisine remains my favorite since it is rich in both variety and flavor and is delicious and healthful.

This book features recipes for traditional Turkish dishes, which utilize a variety of beans, grains, fresh fruits, vegetables, herbs, and of course yogurt (one of Turkey's most important contributions to international cuisine). Vegetables are an integral part of the majority of Turkish recipes. In fact vegetables are considered meals in themselves, usually accompanied by rice or bulgur and served cold or at room temperature. A selection of Anatolian dishes makes a heavenly vegetarian feast!

Since Turkish cooking requires no special equipment, it is generally very easy to prepare. There are also a few recipes in this book that, although a bit challenging, are more than worth the effort.

In Turkey we talk about individuals with "tasty hands." This implies that they have wonderful recipes and are excellent cooks. I hope you will find that I have "tasty hands" and I hope you will acquire some "tasty hands" by preparing my recipes.

I met Sheilah Kaufman at a Turkish luncheon, a program that I organized at our residence to introduce Turkish cuisine to ladies in my Welcome to Washington group. After discovering our mutual love of cooking, we became close friends. When I was encouraged to write down my recipes by our Turkish-American and American friends, but foremost by Sheilah, I wanted to work with her in writing this book. Friends from both groups were very supportive throughout this project.

Sheilah and I tested each recipe in this book together. I have always prepared these dishes by taste and eye measurement. Sheilah taught me to use measurements in my cooking and helped me understand how Americans measure. She worked with me in the preparation of the dishes and recorded the recipes, and gave me enormous support, tireless assistance, and encouragement in this long arduous endeavor. We had a lot of fun working together in the kitchen and I will always be grateful to Sheilah for her endless energy, close cooperation, and valuable contributions.

Nur Ilkin
Washington, D.C., August 2001

History of Turkish Cuisine

"... Food is a mirror that reflects the history and culture of a nation with remarkably little distortion. The ingredients, dishes, and cooking techniques of a cuisine, together with the names used to designate them, all offer abundant clues to the historical growth of a nation..."

—Alya Algar in *Classical Turkish Cooking*

The history of modern Turkey began with people who migrated from the Altay Mountains in Central Asia towards Anatolia (Asia Minor), and who encountered different culinary traditions that they assimilated into their own cuisine. The Turks of historical times led a nomadic life, dependent on agriculture and on the breeding of domestic animals. Central Asian Turks consumed mutton, goat meat, and beef, and the meat was prepared in a *tandir*, an underground oven, or grilled over an open wood or charcoal fire as kebabs. *Kavurma* was another favorite—small cubes of meat cooked in its own fat, salted, stored in large earthenware containers, and eaten in the winter months. *Pastirma*, a preserved meat, was salted and spiced and dried in the sun. These foods are still a very popular part of Turkish cuisine. Interestingly enough, most Turkish food is prepared on top of the stove. The oven is hardly used.

Milk and dairy products had a special place in the nomadic diet. Mare's milk in particular was valued over sheep or cow's milk. Nutritionists have pointed out that mare's milk has four times more vitamin C than cow's milk. The milk was simmered in large shallow pans and the cream, which rose to the surface and formed a crust, was widely consumed. The remaining milk was then dried in the sun and stored as powder. Milk and thick cream were the basic elements in a nomad's breakfast. Mare's milk was also fermented to make a strong alcoholic beverage known as *kimiz*, which is still widely consumed among the Turkish peoples of Central Asia. The Turkish diet consisted primarily of yogurt, which is regarded as one of the most famous Turkish culinary contributions to the world.

Basic foods also included wheat and barley. Boiled, dried, and cracked wheat is called *bulgur*, and is still an important cereal in the nutrition of Turkish people. Flour, salt, and water formed dough that was rolled out in round layers and browned on a thin iron plate, dried, and stored. This *yufka ekmek* (yufka bread) is still made the same way in Anatolia.

Chinese and Mongolian influences to Turkish cuisine include homemade noodles and *manti* (like tortellini). The Uyghurs (mid-eighth century) were strongly influenced in their culture by China, and it is probably during this period that manti became part of the Turkish diet. But the Chinese borrowed from the Turks adding the use of stuffed dishes to their cuisine.

Fresh fruits were consumed in season and dried for winter months. To sweeten fruits, they were soaked and cooked in water and molasses (made from grape juice).

Maurice Asseo

FRUITS AND VEGETABLES IN THE INDOOR MARKET

Even with the advancements in technology and agriculture, many of the methods of food production—preserving, cooking, and baking—are still in use in rural areas of Turkey. It is interesting to note that even today Turkish cuisine holds a place of its own, resisting the encroachment of fast food in the home and in restaurants.

Many other cultures have left their mark on Turkish cuisine. Arab influences, especially in the south and southeastern parts of Anatolia included many spices—hot peppers in particular. The Persian, Hittite, and Byzantine Empires introduced different vegetables like cabbage, cauliflower, and parsley—all of Mediterranean origin. Turkish cuisine was greatly influenced by the Iranians use of a combination of meats and fruits in their stews as well as vegetable stews (*yakhni*). The word "kebab" is of Persian origin. *Pilav* (pilaf) is the Turkish version of *pulau* (Persian). This confluence of Turkish and Iranian elements gradually led to a cuisine that the Moghuls transplanted to India, where it was enhanced and changed.

During the rise of the Ottoman Empire the culinary arts played an important part in court life, with the richest and most diverse flavors found in dishes prepared during the reign of Sultan Mehmet the Second, who conquered Istanbul in 1453. This enhancing of the culinary arts began (before the Ottomans arrived) with the Seljuqs, their cultural forebear. The introduction, in Anatolia, of many new foods included fruits, vegetables, and herbs that had been nonexistent in Central Asia as well as new sources of olive oil and seafood. It was not long before these new ingredients combined with the established foods like breads, dough products, and kebabs, to yield many new dishes. By the beginning of the 1700s, the sultan's kitchen staff encompassed 1,370 people, all of them housed within the palace grounds. The preparation of each type of dish (soups, kebabs, pilafs, vegetables, fish, breads, pastries, candy, jams, etc.) was regarded as a separate skill. Alya Algar, in *Classical Turkish Cooking*, notes that "In 1661, a list showed that 36,000 bushels of rice, 3,000 pounds of noodles, 500,000 bushels of chickpeas, and 12,000 pounds of salt were used in the palace; and in 1723, the annual meat supply of the palace was 30,000 head of beef, 60,000 of mutton, 20,000 of veal, 200,000 fowl, 100,000 pigeons."

Dalia Carmel

As time passed, olive oil gradually became an alternative for butter, and sugar replaced honey and grape molasses in desserts. Cumin, coriander, cinnamon, mustard, pepper, and saffron were the foremost spices used. Parsley, mint leaves, onions, and garlic were the primary herbs and seasonings.

In Anatolia, the Turks were now neighbors of the Greeks, and some Greek influence was felt, especially in the baking of round loaves of bread as opposed to the flat breads of Central Asia. In addition, from the eleventh to the fourteenth centuries, many words of Greek origin were applied to fish and seafood dishes.

Today there are seven regions in Turkey, each with indigenous agricultural products,

OLIVES

cultures, customs, traditions, and local dishes. A same dessert made in the Black Sea area with hazelnuts, would contain pistachio nuts if made in the southeast region of Turkey.

Neşet Eren summed up Turkish cuisine best in *The Art of Turkish Cooking*: "Many of the well-known national cuisines rely on one basic element. For instance, French cuisine is based on the sauce. Pasta forms the essence of the Italian cuisine. There is, however, no single dominant feature in the Turkish kitchen. Meats, fish, vegetables, pastries, and fruit are cooked in an infinite variety of ways."

Ogier Ghislain de Busbecq, a sixteenth-century ambassador, remarked of Istanbul, "Nature seems to have created this place as the capital of the world." Since Istanbul was the capital of the huge Ottoman Empire, was so well situated it became geographically the marketplace for a large assortment and variety of food products and spices that came from as far away as Wallachia and Yemen via the Bosphorous and the Dardanelles.

Meal Times

Turkish people eat three meals a day. Breakfast consists usually of eggs, a variety of cheeses (white Turkish cheese is a must), olives, freshly baked bread, a variety of homemade jams and butter, and tea. Lunch is traditionally a hot meal eaten at home by the entire family, and dinner is the main meal of the day. In winter, dinner usually begins with hot soup, followed by a meat (poultry or fish) dish with vegetables or legumes. Pickles are served as an accompaniment in the winter, and fresh salad is served in the summer. Olive oil dishes appear after the main course as accompaniments, and are served hot or cold, and as many as two or three may be served at one meal. Boerek (filled pastries) are sometimes served in place of a hot main dish, but are also used for breakfast and snacks. When properly served, side dishes are always presented and eaten in separate dishes and always have their own plate since they deserve to be enjoyed individually. Bread is served with all dishes except manti and boerek.

Desserts are usually fruits in season, puddings, or compotes. Syrupy pastry desserts are usually reserved for parties or an occasional treat with tea or coffee.

Dalia Carmel

RESTAURANT IN ISTANBUL

Guide to Ingredients

Aleppo Pepper: Sweet and sharp chili from the Aleppo region of Syria, with moderate heat that doesn't overpower its fruity flavor. Can be substituted by using four parts sweet paprika plus one part cayenne pepper.

Maurice Asseo

LADY IN MARKET

Arugula (also known as rocket or roquette): A leafy green vegetable used with fish dishes and a main ingredient in salads.

Boerek: Thinly rolled pastry, often a paper-thin variety called *yufka*, wrapped around a variety of fillings or layered. The many different types of boerek can be fried, baked, cooked on a griddle, or broiled. The most popular fillings are cheese, meat, spinach, and potatoes. If properly made, boereks should be light and crisp with no trace of excess oil. It is said that no girl should marry before mastering the art of making these pastries.

Celeriac (celery root): A plant closely related to celery that develops a knobby baseball-size root with a crisp texture and intense celery flavor. The best ones for cooking are small, firm, and heavy. They should be free of dents, cuts, or soft spots and the leaves, if attached, should be fresh and green. Scrub them well before using. Cooked celeriac and potato complement each other and are often combined in one dish.

Clarified Butter: A pure butter concentrate made by slowly melting butter on very low heat. One pound of butter yields 11 to 13 ounces of clarified butter. To make approximately 2 to 3 cups of clarified butter melt 5 sticks of butter in a pan over very low heat until a foam appears on the surface. Do not scorch or burn the butter. Skim off the foamy top. It takes about 10 minutes per pound of butter to clarify. Pour the clarified butter into a bowl. Discard the milk solids that gather at the bottom of the pan. Cover and refrigerate until ready to use.

Dalia Carmel

DRIED PEPPERS IN MARKET

Cubanel peppers: These long, thin, green peppers are similar to Anaheim peppers, but slightly less flavorful. They are classified as sweet peppers.

Dill: An herb with a slightly anise flavor that complements all types of salads, especially cucumber. It is an excellent addition to sauces for fish, eggs, and cheese.

Doner Kebap: Thinly sliced marinated lamb that is rotated and cooked on a vertical spit, then cut in very thin slices and served with pita bread.

Dolmas: A variety of vegetables from tomatoes to eggplant that are stuffed with a filling of minced meat and herbs (these are eaten hot) or rice and herbs (these are eaten cold). Dolmas also include fillings wrapped with cabbage leaves or grape leaves.

Kasseri Cheese: This sheep's or goat's milk has a sharp, salty flavor and hard texture similar to that of cheddar.

Kebabs: Almost every district in Anatolia has its own kebab specialty! Made from plain or marinated meat (usually lamb) that is either grilled or stewed and consists of cubes cooked on skewers and grilled over a charcoal fire. Usually chunks of tomato, green pepper, and onion alternate with the chunks of meat.

Köfte: Finely minced meat combined with spices, onions, and other ingredients that are filled and shaped then grilled, fried, broiled, or baked. They usually have the shape of a lemon but are named according to the cooking method used and the shape or ingredients.

When plump, dipped in egg, and fried, they have the marvelous name of Ladies' Thighs (*kadin budu*)! Sometimes they are cooked and served in sauce.

Mezzes: Appetizers or hors d'oeuvres, originally served to appease the appetite before the main meal. Now used for snacks or depending on the dish served with meals, as a side dish. Examples include pastirma, hummus, eggplant dishes, and dips.

Mint: A fragrant herb used in salads, with lamb, fresh peas, new potatoes, as a garnish, or as a tea.

Muhallebi: A type of pudding made with milk, sugar, and ground rice.

Oregano: A strong, aromatic herb that is an essential ingredient in tomato sauces or tomato dishes, stews, or meats, and blends well with basil.

Okra: A vegetable thought to have originated in Ethiopia and spread to North Africa and the Middle East before reaching America. Its flavor and texture are unique, and its taste is somewhere between that of eggplant and asparagus. It goes well with other vegetables, especially tomatoes, peppers, and onions. When cooked, it gives off a juice that thickens any liquid to which it is added, which explains its longstanding use in soups and stews.

SPICES

Parsley: An herb with several varieties. Freshly chopped flat leaf parsley is used in sauces, salads, soups, and vegetable dishes. An excellent garnish, especially for vegetables. Curly leaf parsley is not grown in many European countries and is not used.

Pilaf: One of the most important dishes at a Turkish table, these are usually made from either rice or bulgur (cracked wheat), lentils, and vermicelli. They can include vegetables like eggplant, chickpeas, beans, or peas. In the past, pilafs were a course by themselves, but now are served as accompaniments to meat or chicken.

Rosemary: A refreshing, pungent herb that is usually sprinkled on roast lamb and other meats. It is also used in marinades.

Sage: A strong, distinctively flavored herb mostly used to make tea.

Dalia Carmel

VEGETABLES IN THE MARKET

Soups: Light or heavy, cold or hot, Turkish cuisine offers a wide variety of soups, which are usually made from a chicken or meat stock. The most popular are lentil soup, yogurt soup, and wedding soup.

Tarragon: An herb used mainly in southeastern Turkey where its fragrant flavor is added to soups, salads, poultry, roasted meats, and fish dishes. It is also used to flavor wine vinegar and salad dressings.

Thyme: A popular seasoning for all soups, stews, casseroles, and sauces. In French cooking it is part of the bouquet garni. It is also used in green salads and tomato dishes.

Turkish zucchini: These pale green zucchini are available at farmer's markets. They are about 6 inches long, and ideal for stuffing.

Aşure is a pudding made of grains, legumes, fruits, nuts, sugar, and spices. It is sometimes called "Noah's pudding."

Ayran is a drink made of yogurt beaten with cold water and a dash of salt. Sometimes milk is used. Similar to buttermilk, it is very refreshing on a hot day.

THE BAKER

Bazlama is a type of round bread, traditionally baked in a tandir or between two thin hot iron plates.

Beyaz peynir is the most popular Turkish medium soft type of cheese soaked in brine. It is similar to feta, and referred to here as "white Turkish cheese."

Bulgur is a cooked, dried, and partly debranned cracked wheat. Usually used in pilafs and dolmas.

Çökelek is a creamy soft cheese similar to cottage cheese.

Çörek is a crisp flaky pastry with or without any boerek filling used for breakfast or served for snack or with tea.

Erişte is any kind of homemade noodle.

Helva is a sweet dessert made of flour and semolina with butter, sugar, milk, and nuts.

Hoşaf is any dessert made with dried fruit or fruits soaked and cooked in sugar water. It can be made with or without nuts.

13

Maurice Asseo

CRUSTIE'S BAKERY

Kadayif is a readymade finely shredded pastry used to make desserts filled with nuts, clotted cream, or unsalted cheese.

Kimiz is the Turkish word for koumiss, a fermented mare's milk drink.

Kurut is a dried form of yogurt used during winter months in dishes in rural areas.

Leblebi are roasted chickpeas used like salted nuts in appetizers.

Lokum is another name for the candy called Turkish Delight in western countries.

Manti are similar to ravioli; filled dough that is boiled.

Oruk is a type of ground meat mixed with bulgur and spiced and cooked on skewers or as oval patties similar to hamburgers.

Oturtma is a dish similar to stuffed vegetables, usually made from eggplant or summer squash.

Pekmez is a type of molasses made from grapes or other fruits and used to sweeten desserts.

Pide is a flattened round bread usually used during Ramadan.

Piyaz refers to any type of dried legume salad served with hardcooked eggs and vegetables.

Sarma is any dish of wrapped grape leaves, cabbage, or Swiss chard with a filling.

Sucuk is preserved meat similar to pepperoni and made from ground lamb or beef.

Surup is the Turkish word for syrup.

Tahini is roasted and ground sesame seeds. The taste is similar to peanut butter but thinner in consistency. A substitute for a cup of tahini would be ⅔ cup peanut butter mixed with ⅓ cup oil.

Tandır is a brick oven in the wall or ground that certain dishes are cooked in. They are still used in rural areas of Turkey.

Yufka are readymade pastry leaves, but if you cannot find them, 2 sheets of phyllo dough can be substituted for each sheet of yufka the recipe calls for. It is only used to make boereks.

Dalia Carmel

FRESH FISH FROM ISTANBUL MARKET

Dalia Carmel

MARKET IN ANKARA

Appetizers:
Mezzes and Starters

Black Sea Cornmeal Cooked With Cheese

8 tablespoons butter

1 to 1⅓ cups cornmeal

1 teaspoon salt

½ pound mozzarella, cut in 1-inch chunks, at room temperature

SERVES 4 TO 6

Cornmeal recipes are always associated with the Black Sea. This can be used as starter, main course, or side dish. It is rich and nourishing, and is a Turkish version of polenta. It is usually served with buttermilk and is quick to prepare (it just takes about 15 minutes).

Melt the butter in a 10-inch skillet until it is bubbly but not brown. Remove pan from heat and stir in cornmeal and salt, mixing well. Return pan to high heat and add 1 cup of cold water, whisking constantly until butter is absorbed. Reduce heat to medium-high, and constantly whisking gradually add another 1 cup of cold water. Slowly, using a wooden spoon and stirring constantly, add another cup of cold water stirring until it is all absorbed. Shake the pan around in a circular and back-and-forth motion. Mixture should be boiling around the edges.

Drop in the chunks of cheese and press them in with a wooden spoon so they sit on the bottom of the pan in the cornmeal. Continue to shake the pan in a circular and back-and-forth motion over medium-high heat. Keep pressing on the pieces of cheese. As soon as the cheese melts, remove the pan from the heat and serve.

Appetizers: Mezzes and Starters

Cabbage Leaves Stuffed With Rice

ZEYTİNYAĞLI LAHANA DOLMASI

I cup uncooked medium-grain white rice

½ cup extra-virgin olive oil

I pound onions, finely chopped

4 tablespoons pine nuts

4 tablespoons currants, washed

2 teaspoons sugar

3 tablespoons salt

½ teaspoon pepper

½ teaspoon ground allspice

½ bunch Italian parsley, washed and finely chopped with stems

½ bunch dill, washed and finely chopped with stems

2 teaspoons dried mint

3 small cabbages (I½ pounds each)

I onion, sliced

I lemon, peeled and sliced crosswise

I teaspoon salt

¼ cup olive oil

Soak the rice in water for about 20 minutes then drain well and set aside.

In a saucepan heat the oil, add the onions, and sauté about 10 minutes on medium heat, constantly stirring. Add the rice and pine nuts and sauté another 5 to 6 minutes, stirring. Then add currants, sugar, 2 teaspoons of the salt, pepper, allspice, parsley, dill, and mint, mixing well. Add I cup of water, cover, and simmer until all the water is absorbed. Set aside to cool.

With a sharp knife cut out the cores of cabbages.

In a large 6- to 8-quart pot, boil 4 quarts of water with 6 teaspoons salt, and drop in a cabbage. Turn it periodically and push it down with a spoon. Cook the cabbage 10 minutes, stirring and separating the leaves. Remove the leaves and place them in a large pot of cold water. Repeat with the other cabbages. Drain the cabbages. Trim I inch from the bottom of each leaf and carefully slice off pieces from the thick ribs without cutting the leaf.

Place the ribs facing down on the work surface and place a tablespoon of rice filling along the bottom edge of every leaf. Fold the sides over the filling and roll up the leaf. Repeat with remaining leaves and filling. If the leaves are large cut them vertically. Save any torn or unused leaves. Place some of the extra leaves on the bottom of a large sauté pan, add sliced onions, and place the rolled cabbage on the onions. When the first layer is done you can make a second layer and a third layer if necessary. Place lemon slices on the last cabbage layer. Cover the stuffed cabbage with any remaining leaves. Pour on 2 cups of water, 1 teaspoon salt, and oil. Place a plate upside down on the rolled leaves to weigh them down.

Bring water to a boil, reduce heat, cover, and simmer 45 to 50 minutes. Set aside. When cool enough, refrigerate. Serve cold the next day with lemon quarters.

Appetizers: Mezzes and Starters

21

Carrots With Garlic and Yogurt

7 tablespoons extra-virgin olive oil

I medium onion, finely chopped

I pound carrots, coarsely grated

3 to 4 cloves garlic

½ teaspoon salt

I cup Drained Yogurt (page 42)

2 teaspoons Aleppo pepper or paprika

Olives, optional

SERVES 8

Carrots will never be the same after you've eaten this dish! Turkish zucchini can be used instead of the carrots, but a teaspoon of dried mint needs to be added to the dish.

In a 3-quart pot, heat 5 tablespoons of the oil and sauté the onions, stirring over medium heat for 5 minutes. Do not let them brown or burn. Add the carrots, stirring to mix well, and continue cooking for 10 minutes. Remove from heat and let cool.

Crush the garlic and salt in a mortar and pestle. Place the cooled carrots in a large bowl and add the drained yogurt and the garlic mixture. Mix well and place in a serving dish. Combine the remaining 2 tablespoons of olive oil and the paprika and drizzle in a design over the top of the carrots, decorate with olives if desired. Serve at room temperature or chilled.

Eggplant Salad With Olive Oil

3 eggplants, stems trimmed
and leaves removed

Juice of 1 lemon

1/4 cup extra-virgin olive oil

1 clove garlic, minced

1/4 to 1/2 teaspoon salt

SERVES 6

Pierce the skin of the eggplants all around with the tip of a small sharp knife. Cook over an open flame (a charcoal fire is preferable but gas will do), turning occasionally, until the skin is charred and the flesh has softened. Or broil about 8 inches from the broiler heat for 25 minutes or until soft.

Using the flat side of the blade of a knife, gently tap all around the eggplants. With a sharp knife, carefully peel the skin off the eggplants from top to bottom while it is hot. Cut eggplants diagonally in 1/2-inch slices, remove the stems, and discard.

In a large bowl, mix 2 cups of water with half the lemon juice. Place the eggplants in the water for a few minutes to cool. Place eggplants in a fine sieve and drain well, pushing the eggplants with a wooden spoon.

In a bowl whisk together the olive oil, remaining lemon juice, garlic, and salt. Whisk into drained eggplant, cover, and chill. Serve cold.

Appetizers: Mezzes and Starters

Eggplant Salad With Yogurt

YOĞURTLU PATLICAN SALATASI

3 eggplants, stems trimmed
and leaves removed

Juice of ½ lemon

1 cup Drained Yogurt
(page 42)

2 to 3 cloves garlic, minced

½ teaspoon salt

SERVES 8 TO 10 AS A DIP

This can also be used as a dip.

Pierce the skin of the eggplants all around with the tip of a small sharp knife. Cook over an open flame (a charcoal fire is preferable but gas will do), turning occasionally, until the skin is charred and the flesh has softened. Or broil about 8 inches from the broiler heat for 25 minutes or until soft.

In a large bowl, mix 2 cups of water with lemon juice.

With the flat side of a knife blade, lightly tap all around the eggplants. While still hot, hold the eggplants by their stems and using a small sharp knife, remove the peel from top to bottom. Cut eggplants diagonally in ½-inch slices, cut off the stems and discard, and place eggplants in the bowl of water. Repeat with each eggplant. Place eggplants in a fine sieve and strain well, pushing the eggplants with a wooden spoon.

In a bowl, whisk together the yogurt, garlic, and salt. Mix with eggplant, cover, and chill. Serve cold with roasted pita bread, crackers and vegetables.

Eggplant With Tahini

This can also be used as a dip or salad.

3 eggplants, stems trimmed
  and leaves removed

Juice of 1 lemon

¼ cup sesame paste (tahini)

3 cloves garlic

1 teaspoon salt

GARNISH:

2 tablespoons extra-virgin
  olive oil

1 teaspoon Aleppo pepper

SERVES 8 TO 10

Pierce the skin of the eggplants all around with the tip of a small sharp knife.

Cook the eggplants over an open flame, turning occasionally until the skin is charred and the flesh has softened. A charcoal fire is preferred, but gas will do. Or broil about 8 inches from the broiler for 25 minutes, turning, until soft.

In a large bowl, mix 2 cups of water with ½ of the lemon juice.

With the flat side of a knife blade, lightly tap all around the eggplants while turning them. Then, while the eggplants are still hot, hold each eggplant by its stem and, using a small sharp knife, remove the peel from top to bottom. Cut the eggplants diagonally in ½-inch slices, cut off the stems and discard, and place the eggplants in the bowl of lemon water.

Remove the eggplants from the water, drain well, and place the eggplants in a fine sieve over a bowl. Strain the eggplants into a bowl by pushing them through the sieve using a wooden spoon.

Add the sesame paste, remaining lemon juice, garlic and salt, and mix well. Place in a serving dish.

In a small bowl mix the oil and the Aleppo pepper together and drizzle over the eggplant mixture. Cover, chill, and serve.

Appetizers: Mezzes and Starters

Fried Eggplant

2 eggplants, peeled in stripes about ¼ inch wide

Salt

1½ cups vegetable oil

SERVES 4 TO 6

This can be served with a favorite Tomato Sauce (page 40) or Yogurt Sauce (page 43).

Slice the peeled eggplants into ¼-inch-wide slices. Sprinkle with salt and let them sit in a colander in the sink for 2 hours. Wash the slices of eggplant to remove any salt. Gently dry the slices so no water remains on them (water and boiling oil do not mix well).

Place the oil in a large skillet and heat for 10 minutes. Test a slice of eggplant to see if it begins to brown and the oil bubbles around it when immersed. Place some of the slices in the oil and fry, turning occasionally until the slices are golden brown on both sides, 2 to 4 minutes per side. Remove fried eggplant slices from the pan and drain well on paper towels. Fry remaining eggplant slices. Drain well and serve.

Fried Zucchini

3 long zucchini

Salt

½ cup all-purpose flour

1½ cups vegetable oil

SERVES 4

This recipe is very similar to tempura.

Cut the zucchini in half horizontally, peel them, and slice them horizontally into ⅛-inch-thick slices. Salt the zucchini and let sit in a bowl of water for 40 minutes. Wash well to remove salt, drain, and gently pat dry.

In a large bowl mix ½ cup water with the flour and stir to make a thick paste. Place the zucchini in the paste and mix well.

In a large skillet, heat the oil for 5 to 10 minutes. Remove zucchini from the paste and place some in the hot oil. Do not crowd the pan. Fry, turning, until the pieces are golden brown. Drain well on paper towels. Serve with Yogurt Sauce (page 43).

Appetizers: Mezzes and Starters

Grape Leaves Stuffed With Rice

ZEYTİNYAĞLI YAPRAK DOLMASI

I cup uncooked medium-grain white rice

I (16-ounce) jar grape leaves, drained

¾ cup extra-virgin olive oil

I pound onions, finely chopped

4 tablespoons pine nuts

4 tablespoons currants, washed

2 teaspoons sugar

2½ teaspoons salt

½ teaspoon pepper

½ teaspoon ground allspice

½ bunch Italian parsley, washed, finely chopped with stems

½ bunch dill, washed and finely chopped with stems

2 teaspoons dried mint

I large onion, sliced

I lemon, peeled and sliced crosswise

Soak the rice in salted water for 20 minutes then drain well.

Place 5 cups of water in a saucepan and bring to a boil. Open the rolled leaves and place all leaves in boiling water and cook for 2 minutes. Transfer to a colander using a slotted spoon and drain. Separate the leaves and remove stems and set aside.

In a saucepan heat ½ cup of the oil and sauté the chopped onions for 10 minutes on medium heat, constantly stirring. Add rice and pine nuts, sauté another 5 to 6 minutes, stirring. Add currants, sugar, 2 teaspoons of the salt, pepper, allspice, parsley, dill, and dried mint. Mix well and add I cup of water, cover, and simmer until all the water is absorbed. Set aside to cool.

Take a grape leaf, vein side up, put 2 teaspoons of rice filling along the bottom edge of a leaf, fold sides over the filling and roll up the leaf. Continue the same way with the remaining leaves. If leaves are too large, cut them vertically. Do not throw away any damaged or unused ones.

Place some of the extra leaves on the bottom of a large sauté pan and add sliced onions. Place the rolled grape leaves next. When the bottom of the pan is filled, start the next layer on top of the first, and a third on top if necessary. Cover them with the remaining grape leaves and place lemon slices on top. Place a plate upside down over the leaves. Add ¼ cup oil, the remaining

$\frac{1}{2}$ teaspoon salt, and 2 cups water. Bring to a boil, cover, reduce heat to simmer, and simmer 1 hour. Remove from heat.

When cooled, refrigerate. Garnish with lemon quarters before serving.

Hot Olive Balls With Cheese Pastry

48 small pimento-stuffed
  green olives

2 cups grated cheddar cheese

8 tablespoons butter, softened
  to room temperature

1 cup all-purpose flour
  (more if needed)

½ teaspoon salt, optional
  (don't use if the cheese is
  very salty)

1 teaspoon Aleppo pepper

MAKES 4 DOZEN BALLS

This recipe is from Mrs. Tuygan.

Drain the olives in a sieve, then place on paper towels to get rid of any remaining liquid. In a large bowl combine the cheese, butter, flour, salt (if using), and Aleppo pepper. Using your hands, mix until dough is formed (but try not to overwork it), and you have a smooth ball. If dough is too sticky, add a little more flour.

Pinch off a teaspoon of dough, roll it into a ball with the palms of your hands, then take a finger and flatten it. Place an olive in the middle, encase it, and roll the dough around in-between your palms until a rounded ball is formed. Pinch off any excess dough so balls are about ¾-inch across. Continue until all the olives and dough are used. Place the balls on a cookie sheet and place in the freezer until the balls are firm, 20 to 30 minutes.

Preheat oven to 400°F.

Bake directly from the freezer without thawing for about 15 minutes or until balls are golden brown. If not baking immediately, place olive balls in freezer bags and keep frozen until ready to use.

30   Taste of Turkish Cuisine

Hummus

1 pound dried chickpeas (you can use canned)

1 to 2 teaspoons salt

6 cloves garlic, finely chopped

½ to 1 cup freshly squeezed lemon juice (2 to 4 lemons)

½ cup sesame paste (tahini)

2 tablespoons vegetable oil

½ teaspoon paprika

½ teaspoon ground cumin

SERVES 12 TO 15

This recipe needs to be started the day before if you are using dried chickpeas.

Soak the chickpeas in water overnight with the salt if using dried chickpeas. In the morning, place them in a pot with the same water and bring to a boil. Reduce heat to medium, and partially cover the pot, or use a pressure cooker. Cook over medium heat for 50 to 60 minutes or more (or use a pressure cooker for 30 minutes), remove from the heat, and strain. Save the cooking liquid and set aside. If using canned chickpeas, just rinse well and drain.

Place the chickpeas in a food processor with the garlic and ½ cup of lemon juice, the tahini, and ¼ cup of the reserved cooking liquid. Puree. If mixture is too thick, add a little more of the reserved cooking liquid and puree again. Place the hummus in a shallow serving dish and spread it out using the back of a wet metal spoon.

Combine the vegetable oil, paprika, and cumin in a small bowl. Drizzle over the top of the hummus. Serve with bread or crackers.

Jerusalem Artichokes With Vegetables

1 pound Jerusalem artichokes

¼ cup extra-virgin olive oil

1 large onion, finely chopped

2 small carrots, sliced cross-wise into ¼-inch slices

6 to 7 stems Italian parsley, finely chopped

1 large tomato, peeled and chopped

Salt

½ teaspoon sugar

1½ tablespoons uncooked medium-grain white rice

GARNISH:
1 tablespoon finely chopped fresh Italian parsley

SERVES 4

Peel the Jerusalem artichokes with a peeler and cut in them in half if large (mine were twice the size of a walnut), wash, and drain.

In a saucepan heat the olive oil and sauté the onions for 5 to 6 minutes, add carrots, chopped parsley stems, and tomatoes. Stir to mix well. Add salt, sugar, rice, Jerusalem artichokes, and 1½ cups of water. Bring to a boil, cover, and cook over medium heat 30 to 35 minutes. Remove from heat and let cool. Sprinkle with chopped parsley. Eat at room temperature.

Leeks, Carrots, and Rice in Olive Oil

1 ½ pounds leeks

⅓ cup extra-virgin olive oil

1 medium onion, chopped fine

2 carrots, cut crosswise in ¼-inch slices

1 heaping tablespoon uncooked medium-grain white rice

Salt

GARNISH:

1 tablespoon chopped parsley

1 lemon, cut lengthwise into 4 sections

SERVES 4

*T*rim leeks by removing the outer leaf, trimming the tips off the bottoms, and cutting leeks and most of the green into crosswise 1-inch slices. Place leeks in a large bowl and cover with water. Let sit 10 minutes, then change the water and rinse, repeating until there is no sand in the water. Drain well.

In a 3-quart pot, heat the oil and sauté the onions and carrots. Cook, stirring over medium heat for 5 minutes. Add leeks and sauté for a minute.

Cut a parchment paper circle to fit over the vegetables.

Add the rice to vegetables and 1 ¾ cups of water. Bring to a boil, reduce heat to simmer, cover vegetables with the parchment circle, cover, and cook for 50 minutes.

Sprinkle with parsley and serve with lemon wedges. Eat cold, warm, or at room temperature.

Lemon Sauce

2 egg yolks

Juice of 1 lemon

1 teaspoon all-purpose flour

MAKES ½ TO ¾ CUP

This sauce is not used separately, like a tomato sauce, but is always added to meat, chicken, or vegetable dishes.

Mix all the ingredients together with ½ cup water. Take a ladleful of cooking liquid from the pan in which you are cooking your meat or vegetable and slowly stir the lemon sauce into it, mixing well. Quickly add the lemon sauce/cooking liquid to the pan and whisk constantly to prevent curdling. Boil for a minute and remove from heat.

Mini Cheese Fingers

I pound feta or white Turkish cheese

I egg, separated

¼ cup chopped fresh parsley

¼ cup chopped fresh dill

I-pound package boerek pastry (wedge shaped), cut in half vertically

I to I ½ cups oil

MAKES 70 TO 75

This recipe is another version of the versatile boereks. This recipe makes a lot, but it can be halved. Of course it is nice to always have some of these handy in the freezer.

*I*n a large bowl mix together the cheese, egg yolk, chopped parsley, and dill. Mash/mix the mixture together with your hands to blend well.

Using one half wedge of boerek pastry at a time, place a small dab of the filling at the end with the straight edge, fold the pointed sides over to form 2 triangles over the filling. Carefully roll up the pastry until only 2 to 3 inches of the pointed end are left unrolled. Dip this end in the egg white, finish rolling, and press to seal.

In a 3-quart pot heat enough oil to reach 4 to 5 inches in depth. When oil is hot, drop in a handful of boereks at a time. The oil will sizzle if it is hot enough. Turn once or twice to brown evenly. Cook until golden brown then remove from the oil and drain well on paper towels.

Appetizers: Mezzes and Starters

35

Muska Boerek

SPINACH FILLING:

4 tablespoons vegetable oil

1 large onion, finely chopped

1 pound frozen chopped spinach, thawed and drained well

Salt

Freshly ground pepper

1/4 teaspoon ground nutmeg

1/2 cup white Turkish or feta cheese, crumbled

CHEESE FILLING:

1/2 pound white Turkish or feta cheese, crumbled

1/4 cup grated cheddar cheese

1/2 bunch fresh parsley, finely chopped

1/2 bunch fresh dill leaves, finely chopped

25 sheets spring roll pastry, each cut into 4 vertical strips

2 egg whites

oil for frying

MAKES 100

Use one or both of these fillings to fill the boereks.

Prepare the spinach filling. Heat the oil in a skillet and sauté the onions. Press the spinach gently to make sure there is no liquid left and add to the onions, mixing well. Add salt and freshly ground pepper to taste, and nutmeg, mixing well. Cook, stirring, for 5 to 6 minutes. Remove pan from the heat and when mixture is cool add the cheese and mix well.

Prepare the cheese filling. In a large bowl combine the cheeses, parsley, and dill mixing well.

Take a strip of pastry and place it vertically toward you on a flat work surface. Place a tablespoon of either filling on the bottom right-hand corner of the pastry. Fold the corner over from right to left to form a triangle, then lift the corner on the left side straight up. Now fold over from left to right. The corner is now on the right, so fold it straight up. Continue folding in this manner (this is how an American flag is folded) until an inch of pastry remains. Dip this part of the pastry into the egg whites and finish folding. This will seal the boerek. Repeat this procedure with the remaining pastry until all filling is used up.

In a large pot or electric fryer, place 3 to 4 inches of oil. Heat the oil for about 10 minutes or until the first boerek makes the oil bubble when it is placed in the pot. Fry until golden brown and drain well on paper towels. Serve hot.

Red Bell Pepper Paste

2 pounds red bell peppers, washed, seeded, ribbed, and chopped into chunks

2 tablespoons extra-virgin olive oil, plus additional for topping

1 teaspoon salt

MAKES 1¼ CUPS

In Turkey, after cooking this for half an hour, it is covered and placed out in the sun where the color gets very dark, and it never will spoil after being made this way. Bell pepper paste is used as a substitute for fresh red bell peppers (1 tablespoon equals one fresh bell pepper) or it is used in many recipes including rice, soup, stews, and casserole dishes. It adds color and flavor to the food.

Place the bell peppers in the food processor and puree. Pour the mixture into a 2-quart pot and cook over medium heat for 10 minutes, stirring occasionally. Lower the heat, and continue cooking for about 90 minutes or until almost all the liquid is gone, stirring from time to time.

Turn heat to high, whisk in the oil and salt, mix well, and continue cooking, stirring constantly for 5 to 10 minutes. Remove pot from the heat and let paste cool.

Place paste in a sterilized jar or jars, press it down with the back of a spoon, and cover with ½-inch of extra-virgin olive oil. Seal and refrigerate.

Appetizers: Mezzes and Starters

37

Red Pepper Spread

1 cup Aleppo pepper

1 cup extra-virgin olive oil

1 cup stale bread crumbs (not canned)

1 cup ground walnuts

1 teaspoon sugar

3 to 4 cloves garlic, mashed (using a garlic press)

Salt

Freshly ground pepper

1/2 teaspoon ground cumin

Juice of 1/2 lemon

MAKES 3 CUPS

This recipe is from Gaziantep in South Eastern Turkey. Aleppo pepper flakes are available in Korean or Mediterranean markets.

Soak the Aleppo pepper in 1/2 cup water and let it sit for 10 to 15 minutes or until all the water is absorbed and mixture has a paste-like consistency. Mix well.

Add the olive oil, bread crumbs, and walnuts, mixing well. Add the sugar, garlic, salt and pepper to taste, and cumin, mixing well. Add the lemon juice, mix well, taste, and adjust seasoning if needed.

Serve at room temperature with bread, crackers or pita bread.

Spinach Stems With Walnuts

CEVİZLİ ISPANAK KÖKÜ

2 pounds fresh spinach with roots, and the small leaves between the stem and the larger leaves

1 teaspoon salt

½ cup extra-virgin olive oil

1 large onion, finely chopped

3 cloves garlic, finely chopped

Aleppo pepper

½ cup coarsely chopped walnuts

SERVES 4 TO 6

It was fascinating to learn from Nur about cooking and eating spinach stems as I have only seen spinach leaves in my super-market. Nur learned this from her sister-in-law Fatma Ilkin.

Cut the roots and the tips of the stems off of the spinach, leaving any small leaves on the lower stem, and cut into 2-inch pieces. Remove the large leaves and set aside for another use.

Place the stems into a large bowl with the salt. Swish to mix well and let sit for 10 to 15 minutes, then drain through a colander. Return the roots and stems to the bowl, cover with cold water without salt, and let sit 10 to 15 minutes. Drain and repeat the process two more times, without salt, until there is no sand left in the bowl.

In a large pot, bring 3 quarts of salted water to a boil and cook the roots and stems for 2 to 3 minutes. Drain well and set aside.

In a large skillet, heat the oil and sauté the onions and garlic over medium heat, stirring, for 5 minutes. Don't let the onions and garlic brown. Add the drained roots, stems, small leaves, Aleppo pepper to taste, and cook, stirring, for 10 minutes. Add the nuts and mix well. Remove from heat.

Cool and serve with pita bread, if desired.

Tomato Sauce

DOMATES SOSU

4 tablespoons extra-virgin
   olive oil

3 large tomatoes, peeled and
   finely chopped

Salt

1 teaspoon sugar

3 cloves garlic, minced

1 teaspoon vinegar, optional

MAKES 1 TO 1¼ CUPS

In a skillet heat the oil and add tomatoes. Simmer over medium heat until well cooked (about 10 minutes). Add salt to taste, sugar, and garlic, cook another minute, add the vinegar if using, and turn off the heat. Use for vegetables or anything a tomato sauce would complement.

Yogurt

1 quart milk

3 tablespoons plain yogurt,
at room temperature

MAKES 1 QUART

Since yogurt plays such an important part in Turkish cuisine (everything from sauces to drinks), we have included a recipe so you can make your own. Yogurt is eaten with some cooked foods, vegetables, meat, rice, stuffed dolmas, and used in soups.

Take an old blanket or bath towel, fold it in fourths, and place it in the corner of a kitchen counter. This is going to be a nest for your yogurt. Take a large glass bowl and set it in the middle of the blanket (or bath towel).

Place the milk in a large pot and bring to a boil. Let it boil for 5 to 10 minutes (until a film or skin forms on the top). Remove it from the heat and carefully pour it into the bowl. Let sit uncovered so it can begin to cool down. Mix the yogurt with a few drops of cold water in a small bowl. Let the milk cool to 115°F to 130°F (when you place your little finger in it, it feels hot to the touch but not burning)

Use a wooden spoon to make a hole in the center of the milk. Pour the yogurt into the hole and stir well. Cover the bowl with plastic wrap and then cover the top of the bowl with both sides of the blanket (as well as sides and bottom) and let the mixture sit at room temperature for at least 12 hours or overnight. Do not move it or stir it. Because it sits at room temperature the yogurt will develop a slightly sour or tangy taste. When the time is up, place the yogurt in a container, cover with 4 layers of paper towels (to absorb excess moisture), and refrigerate. Change the paper towels often the first few days. This helps it thicken faster. Use as needed.

Appetizers: Mezzes and Starters

Drained Yogurt

Place double the amount of yogurt needed in a strainer or cheesecloth over a bowl and let sit overnight, or a minimum of 5 to 6 hours. Discard any liquid that drips through. You will end up with half the amount of yogurt you started with, and it will be thicker and more stable.

Yogurt Sauce

2 cloves garlic

1 teaspoon salt

1 cup plain yogurt

MAKES 1 CUP

This can be used with any fried vegetables.

Crush garlic well in a mortar with salt. Add it to the yogurt, mix well, cover, and chill for 20 minutes for flavors to blend.

Yogurt Spread/Dip With Garlic, Dill, and Walnuts

SARMISAKLI CEVİZLİ YOĞURT

1 cup Drained Yogurt (page 42)

6 cloves garlic, minced

1 tablespoon finely chopped fresh dill weed

4 heaping tablespoons finely chopped walnuts

Pinch of salt

1/2 teaspoon paprika

2 teaspoons extra-virgin olive oil

SERVES 4

In a bowl combine the yogurt, garlic, dill, walnuts, and salt. Mix well. In a small bowl combine the paprika and olive oil. Drizzle the paprika mixture over the top of the yogurt mixture and serve with pita bread or crackers.

Nur's Note: I like to add a slice of white bread placed in the processor and made into fine bread crumbs, mixed with 1 or 2 tablespoons of milk to hold the crumbs together. This is just mixed into the yogurt mixture.

Yogurt and White Cheese

HAYDARİ

I cup Drained Yogurt
(page 42)

4 tablespoons grated white
Turkish cheese

2 to 3 cloves garlic, minced

I teaspoon dried mint

I teaspoon finely chopped
fresh dill

¼ cup extra-virgin olive oil

¼ teaspoon cumin

GARNISH:

I teaspoon extra-virgin olive
oil

½ teaspoon Aleppo pepper

MAKES ABOUT I½ CUPS

A wonderful dip with pita bread and/or vegetables.

*I*n a large bowl combine the yogurt, cheese,
garlic, mint, dill, olive oil, and cumin. If
you're going to use it as a dip, or as mezze put
it on a flat mezze plate. Cover and chill.
Before serving mix the oil and Aleppo pepper
and drizzle over the cheese mixture.

Appetizers: Mezzes and Starters

45

Soups

Dried Pea Soup

1 cup dried peas

1 onion, cut and quartered

Salt

Freshly ground pepper

2 tablespoons butter

1 tablespoon all-purpose flour

¼ teaspoon sugar

GARNISH:
Dried or fresh chopped dill

SERVES 4

In a large bowl, soak the dried peas in 4 cups water to cover for 3 hours, then drain well.

In a 4-quart pot, place the drained peas, onion and 5 cups water with salt and pepper to taste. Partially cover and cook over medium heat, skimming off any scum or foam, for 20 to 25 minutes, stirring occasionally. Reduce heat to low, cover the pot, and cook another 20 minutes.

In a pot melt the butter, remove from the heat and quickly whisk in the flour. Cook over medium heat whisking constantly for a minute. Do not let the flour burn. It should be a light beige color. Pour the soup into the butter mixture, stir to mix well, and cook over medium heat, stirring, until soup comes to a boil. Adjust seasoning and stir in the sugar. Mix well, sprinkle with dill and serve hot.

Ezo Bride's Soup

A traditional village soup. A trick Nur taught me when using lentils in soup is to partially cover the pot so the gasses from the lentils can escape and not blow the lid off!

2 cups dried red lentils, washed and drained

1 onion, finely chopped

1/2 cup uncooked medium-grain white rice or bulgur, washed and drained

3 cloves garlic, minced (in a garlic press)

1 tablespoon tomato paste

Juice of 1 lemon

Salt

Freshly ground pepper

TOPPING:

3 tablespoons butter

2 tablespoons dried mint

1 teaspoon Aleppo pepper, optional

SERVES 6 TO 8.

Place the lentils, onion and 8 cups water in a large pot and bring to a boil. Reduce heat to simmer and skim off any scum or foam with a slotted spoon. Add the rice, partially cover, and cook until the rice is done, about 30 minutes. Add the garlic and the tomato paste, mixing well. Add lemon juice, salt and pepper to taste, and place soup in a large serving bowl.

In a small skillet melt the butter until it sizzles, remove from the heat, and stir in the mint and Aleppo pepper, if desired, mixing well. Pour over the soup and serve.

Grandma's Wheat Soup

1 1/2 cups shelled whole wheat

4 cups of yogurt

6 cups of chicken broth or stock

1 egg

1 tablespoon all-purpose flour

Salt

Freshly ground pepper

TOPPING:

3 tablespoons butter

1 tablespoon dried mint

1 teaspoon Aleppo pepper

SERVES 4 TO 6

This is the traditional soup in our family, prepared when special guests come and on special occasions. I have cooked this in every country Baki and I have lived in. Everyone likes it and asks for the recipe.

Soak the wheat overnight in water. Drain well.

Place the yogurt in a sieve lined with cheesecloth and let the excess liquid drain out for a minimum of 5 to 6 hours, or overnight if possible.

Place the wheat in a large pot with the chicken broth and bring to a boil. Reduce the heat to simmer and cook, covered, for 45 to 60 minutes. Remove from the heat and strain the soup. If desired puree in food processor.

Place the strained yogurt in a small pan with the egg and flour, mixing well. This will help prevent curdling. If mixture is too thick you can add 1/4 cup of water. Cook over low heat, stirring constantly until mixture bubbles. Remove from heat and whisk it into the wheat mixture, cooking over low heat and adding more chicken broth or water if soup is too thick. Stir in salt and pepper to taste and adjust seasoning if needed.

In a small skillet melt the butter and when it is hot and sizzles turn the heat off and quickly add the mint and Aleppo pepper, mixing well. Pour in circles on top of the soup.

Nur's Note: It is important that the butter sizzles and the heat is turned off before adding the mint and paprika. This is a hint I learned from my grandmother. This trick keeps the mint green and the pepper red.

Green Lentil Soup With Noodles

ERİSTELİ YEŞİL MERCİMEK ÇORBASI

1 ½ cups dried green lentils

I tablespoon extra-virgin olive oil

I tablespoon butter

2 onions, finely chopped

Salt

Freshly ground pepper

I tablespoon tomato paste

½ teaspoon Red Bell Pepper Paste (page 37), optional

5 cups boiling beef broth or water

I cup fine soup noodles

TOPPING:

3 tablespoons butter

2 tablespoons dried mint

1/4 teaspoon Aleppo pepper

SERVES 4 TO 6

Soften the lentils overnight in water to cover (or 3 to 4 hours).

In a large pot, heat the oil and butter and sauté the onions, salt and pepper to taste, stirring, for 5 minutes. Drain the lentils and add to the onions along with the tomato paste and bell pepper paste, if using. Cook, stirring, for I to 2 minutes.

Remove the pot from the heat, add 3 cups of the boiling broth or water and mix well. Return the pot to the heat, taste and correct seasoning if needed, and bring to a boil. Reduce heat, cover, and simmer for 20 to 25 minutes.

Add remaining 2 cups boiling broth or water and the noodles, stir well, cover and continue cooking another 10 minutes.

In a small skillet heat the butter until it sizzles and stir in the mint and Aleppo pepper. Mix well and remove from the heat. Pour over soup and serve.

Red Lentil Soup

I cup red lentils

5 cups chicken broth, stock, or water

I onion, cut into quarters

4 ½ tablespoons butter

2 tablespoons all-purpose flour

I chicken bouillon cube

Salt, optional

SERVES 4

Place the lentils, broth, and onion in a 2- or 3-quart pot and bring to a boil. Reduce the heat to simmer, partially cover, and cook, stirring occasionally, for 30 minutes. Remove the soup from the heat and strain it by pushing it through a fine sieve using a wooden spoon. Don't forget to wipe off the back of the sieve periodically with the spoon. If needed, add a little water to help push the last of the soup through the sieve.

Rinse out the pot and melt the butter over low heat. Quickly whisk in the flour and continue whisking making a roux (to thicken the soup). Do not let the flour turn dark brown or burn. Remove the pot from the heat and add the strained soup, the bouillon cube, and I cup water. Return the pot to the heat, whisking constantly, cooking on medium heat. If the soup is too thick you can add more hot water or broth. Cook, stirring until the soup begins to boil, then boil for just a minute and remove from the heat. Taste and add salt if needed.

Rice Soup With Tomatoes

1 tablespoon butter

3 tomatoes, peeled, seeded, and chopped in small pieces

6 cups chicken broth, stock, or water

½ cup uncooked medium-grain white rice

3 tablespoons finely chopped fresh parsley

SERVES 4

This is Nur's diet soup. It's filling and easy to digest. After a lot of heavy diplomatic dinners, she omits the butter, cooking the tomatoes for 5 minutes in their own juice. Then she adds water (not broth), rice, and simmers.

In a pot, heat the butter and sauté the tomatoes for 3 to 4 minutes. Add the chicken broth, mixing well, and bring to a boil. Reduce heat to simmer and add the rice. Cover the pot and cook on low heat for 30 minutes. Before serving stir in parsley.

Vermicelli Soup

This is the lightest and most common soup in Turkey. Whenever we have boiled chicken we always use the broth for making this soup and/or rice.

1 tablespoon butter

3 tomatoes, peeled, seeded, and cut into small pieces

4 cups chicken broth or stock (or a mixture of broth and water)

1 cup dried vermicelli

Salt

Freshly ground pepper

GARNISH:
¼ cup finely chopped fresh parsley

Lemon quarters

SERVES 4

*I*n a large pot, heat the butter and sauté the tomatoes for 5 minutes. Add the chicken broth and bring to a boil. Reduce heat to medium and add the vermicelli, salt and pepper to taste, and cook for 10 minutes, stirring occasionally. Remove the pot from the heat and let the soup rest for another 10 minutes.

Serve in bowls garnished with finely chopped parsley and the lemon quarters. If you have any leftover roasted or boiled chicken, cut or shred a cup of the chicken and add it to the soup.

Soups

55

Wedding Soup

1 onion, cut in half

1 carrot, cut in half

2 cloves garlic

1 bay leaf

2 lamb shanks with bones

4 tablespoons butter

5 tablespoons all-purpose flour

Salt

Freshly ground pepper

Juice of ½ lemon

2 egg yolks

TOPPING:

1 tablespoon butter

1 teaspoon Aleppo pepper

SERVES 6

This traditional wedding soup is still served at weddings in Anotalia. It is a delicious soup for special occasions.

*I*n a large pot bring 7 cups of water to a boil, add onion, carrot, garlic, bay leaf, and lamb shanks, and boil 5 to 6 minutes. Remove any scum and cook, covered, over medium low heat, for 1 hour 45 minutes.

When the meat is cooked, drain it, put shanks in a bowl to cool, and reserve the cooking liquid. Measure the cooking liquid and if you don't have 4 cups add enough water to it to make 4 cups.

Melt the butter in a saucepan, whisk in the flour, blending well over low heat for a minute or two to make a roux. Add the cooking liquid, whisking constantly. When it starts bubbling it is done. Remove pan from heat and add salt and pepper to taste.

Discard the shank bones and any fat. Shred the meat into small pieces and add them to the soup.

Mix together the lemon juice and egg yolks. Take a large ladleful of the soup and add slowly to the egg and lemon mixture, whisking constantly. Then pour the mixture back into the soup, boil 1 minute, and turn off the heat.

Heat 1 tablespoon of butter in a small pan and when it sizzles add the Aleppo pepper, pour the mixture over the soup and serve.

Wheat, Chickpea, and Red Lentil Soup

NOHUTLU VE KIRMIZI MERCİMEKLİ BUĞDAY ÇORBASI

½ cup shelled whole wheat

½ cup dried chickpeas

½ cup red lentils

Juice of 1 lemon

1 teaspoon tomato paste

1 teaspoon Red Bell Pepper Paste (page 37)

Salt

Freshly ground pepper

2 cloves garlic, minced

TOPPING:

2 tablespoons butter

1 tablespoon dried mint

1 teaspoon Aleppo pepper

SERVES 6 TO 8

This typical Anatolian soup is very filling and can be used as a lunch meal by itself.

Soak the wheat overnight, together with the chickpeas, in 4 cups of water. Drain well.

Bring 10 cups of water to a boil, add drained wheat and chickpeas, boil 5 minutes. Reduce heat, cover, and simmer for 1½ hours. Add lentils and cook another 20 minutes. Add lemon juice, tomato paste, bell pepper paste, salt and pepper to taste, and garlic and boil for a minute more.

Melt butter in small frying pan and when it starts sizzling turn off the heat, add mint and Aleppo pepper, and mix well. Pour over the soup, mix, and serve.

Wheat Soup With Yogurt and Chickpeas

NOHUT VE YOĞURTLU BUĞDAY ÇORBASI

2 cups shelled whole wheat

1 cup dried chickpeas

2 teaspoons of salt

3 cups Drained Yogurt
(page 42)

1 egg

TOPPING:

3 tablespoons butter

2 tablespoons dried mint

SERVES 8

In Anatolia this soup is a meal by itself. People working in the fields love it. It is filling and nourishing but not heavy, enabling them to keep working the rest of the day.

Soak the wheat and chickpeas separately in water to cover. Add the salt to the chickpea water. Soak both overnight.

Drain the wheat and chickpeas and place in a large pot with 8 cups of water. Bring to a boil and reduce heat to simmer. Cover and cook, stirring occasionally, for 1 hour to 1 ½ hours.

Place the yogurt in a pot on low heat and add the egg, mixing well. Cook the yogurt mixture, whisking constantly until bubbles appear. Whisk yogurt mixture into the soup, stirring constantly over low heat and cook until bubbles appear. If soup is too thick, a little water may be added.

Place the soup in a large serving bowl and prepare topping. In a small skillet heat the butter until it sizzles, then remove from the heat and quickly stir in the mint, mixing well. Pour the mint mixture over the soup and serve. This soup can also be eaten cold.

Yogurt and Rice Soup

5 cups chicken broth (may be substituted with water)

½ cup uncooked medium-grain white rice, washed and drained

SAUCE:

2 cups Drained Yogurt (page 42)

1 egg

1 tablespoon all-purpose flour

Salt

TOPPING:

2 tablespoons butter

1 tablespoon dried mint

1 teaspoon Aleppo pepper

SERVES 6

This is an excellent soup for upset stomachs. You can omit butter and just sprinkle with mint when dieting.

In a 4-quart pot bring 5 cups of chicken broth or water to a boil. Add the rice, reduce heat to simmer, cover, and cook 20 minutes or until rice is done.

Meanwhile prepare the sauce by whisking the yogurt, egg, and flour well in a pan on low heat. Cook, whisking constantly, until it starts bubbling at the surface. Remove from heat and add this to the cooked rice. Stir and cook 2 to 3 more minutes whisking constantly. Turn off the heat and remove pan. Add salt to taste.

Melt butter in a small frying pan. When it sizzles turn off the heat, add mint and Aleppo pepper, mix well, and drizzle over the soup in a circular design and serve.

Soups

Salads

Arugula Salad

1 bunch fresh arugula, washed
  and drained, cut in half

1 large tomato, cut into
  pieces

1 large clove garlic

1/4 teaspoon salt

Juice of 1/4 lemon

1/4 cup extra-virgin olive oil

1 1/2 teaspoons balsamic
  vinegar

SERVES 2 TO 4

This salad is always eaten with fish.

Place the arugula and tomatoes in a serving bowl.

Using a mortar and pestle, crush the garlic and salt together. Place in a small bowl and add the lemon juice, olive oil, and vinegar, mixing well.

Pour the dressing over the salad and let sit until serving. Serve at room temperature.

Beet Salad

5 medium beets, washed, with
   roots, stems, and leaves
   removed

1 large clove garlic

¼ teaspoon salt

Juice of ¼ lemon

¼ cup extra-virgin olive oil

1 ½ teaspoons balsamic
   vinegar

SERVES 2 TO 4

Place the beets in a 3- to 4-quart pot, cover with water, and cook, covered, on high heat until the water boils. Reduce heat to simmer and cook 15 to 20 minutes or until the beets are tender. Remove from heat, cool, and run under cold water. Peel and slice the beets and place in a serving dish.

Using a mortar and pestle, crush the garlic and salt together (this "marriage" makes them taste better). Place in a small bowl and add the lemon juice, olive oil, and vinegar, mixing well.

Pour the dressing over the beets and let sit until serving. Serve at room temperature or chilled.

Black-Eyed Pea Salad

1 cup dried black-eyed peas

1 teaspoon salt

4 spring onions, washed, roots removed, and thinly sliced

1/2 green bell pepper, seeded, ribbed, and finely chopped

1/2 red bell pepper, seeded, ribbed, and finely chopped

1/2 bunch fresh Italian parsley, washed, dried, and finely chopped

DRESSING:
Juice of 1/2 lemon

2 teaspoons white vinegar

1/2 teaspoon salt

1/2 teaspoon sugar

1/2 cup extra-virgin olive oil

GARNISH:
2 hard-cooked eggs, sliced

SERVES 4 TO 6

Soak the peas in hot water to cover for 2 to 3 hours then drain well.

Place the peas in a 3-quart saucepan with 3 cups of water and the salt, cover partially, and bring to a boil. Lower heat to simmer and cook 20 minutes or more until tender. Drain and cool.

In a large bowl place cooked peas and add spring onions, bell peppers, and parsley. Mix well.

In a small bowl whisk together the lemon juice, vinegar, salt, sugar, and oil. Pour over pea mixture and toss to mix and combine. Garnish with egg slices and serve.

Salads

Bulgur Salad

½ cup fine bulgur

¼ cup hot water

2 bunches fresh Italian pars-ley, finely chopped

1 bunch fresh mint, finely chopped

5 spring onions, whites and greens, thinly sliced

2 small green bell peppers (or 1 large), very finely sliced and cut into small cubes

3 tomatoes, seeded and cut in small pieces

½ teaspoon salt

Juice of 2 lemons

¼ cup extra-virgin olive oil

SERVES 4

A very healthful salad, it can also be used for a light lunch.

Soak the bulgur in the hot water, cover, and let it rest for about 10 minutes.

Place bulgur in a large serving bowl and mix with the parsley, mint, onions, and bell pep-pers. Add the tomatoes, salt, lemon juice, and olive oil. Mix well with the bulgur. Serve at room temperature.

Chickpea Salad

1 (15-ounce) can chickpeas, rinsed and drained

1 medium-size red onion, finely chopped

1/2 green bell pepper, seeded, ribbed, and finely chopped

1/2 red bell pepper, seeded, ribbed, and finely chopped

1/2 bunch fresh Italian parsley, washed, dried, and finely chopped

DRESSING:
Juice of 1/2 lemon

2 teaspoons white vinegar

1/2 teaspoon salt

1/2 teaspoon sugar

1/2 cup extra-virgin olive oil

GARNISH:
2 hard-cooked eggs, sliced

SERVES 4

Place chickpeas in a large bowl and add onions, bell peppers, and parsley. Mix well.

In a small bowl whisk together the lemon juice, vinegar, salt, sugar, and oil. Pour over pea mixture and toss to mix and combine. Garnish with egg slices and serve.

Grandma Fatima's Mung Bean Salad

MAŞ PİYAZI

5 spring onions, washed and wiped dry, white and green parts or 1 clove garlic, finely chopped

1 cup dried mung beans (available at Korean, Mediterranean, or Eastern markets)

½ cup finely chopped fresh Italian parsley

1 teaspoon Aleppo pepper

Salt

4 tablespoons lemon juice (or to taste) (1 to 2 lemons)

3 tablespoons fresh pomegranate seeds, if available

SERVES 6

In the old days in Gaziantep, the ladies took this salad with them when they went to the Turkish baths. They rolled it up in flat bread (yufka) and ate it like a sandwich.

Slice the green onions very very thin.

Wash the mung beans well to remove any impurities. Place beans in a pot, cover with cold water, and bring to a boil. Reduce heat, cover pot, and cook over medium heat for 30 to 45 minutes or until mung beans are tender. Skim off any scum that appears and discard.

Drain the beans and place in a large serving bowl. Combine the cooked mung beans, onions or garlic, parsley, Aleppo pepper, salt to taste, and lemon juice. Adjust seasoning if needed. Sprinkle the pomegranate seeds, if using, over the salad, chill, and serve.

Green Lentil Salad

1 cup green lentils

1 bunch spring onions
  (5 pieces), thinly sliced
  crosswise

1/4 teaspoon salt

1/2 bunch fresh Italian parsley, finely chopped

1 green bell pepper, seeded,
  ribbed, and sliced

DRESSING:

1/4 cup fresh lemon juice
  (1 to 2 lemons)

1/3 cup extra-virgin olive oil

1 teaspoon salt

GARNISH:

2 hard-cooked eggs, optional

6 or more black olives

SERVES 4 TO 6

An ideal healthful lunch dish for a vegetarian or a terrific side dish.

Soak the lentils in water for 3 to 4 hours.

Place the lentils in a 3-quart pot and cover with water. Bring to a boil, reduce heat, and cook, uncovered, for 20 to 25 minutes. Drain well and let cool.

Place the onions, salt, parsley, bell pepper, and cooled lentils in a salad bowl.

In a small bowl whisk together the lemon juice, olive oil, and salt. Pour the dressing over the vegetables and mix well. Garnish with eggs, if using, and olives. Serve at room temperature.

Green Olive Salad

3 cups green cracked olives, pitted or pimento-stuffed

4 medium-size green onions, whites and greens, coarsely chopped

1 bunch fresh Italian parsley, chopped

1 cup finely chopped walnuts

Freshly ground pepper

1 teaspoon Aleppo pepper

1 1/2 tablespoons lemon juice

1/4 cup extra-virgin olive oil

5 to 6 tablespoons pomegranate seeds, optional

SERVES 6 TO 8

This dish comes from Gaziantep province and is usually served wrapped in yufka bread or pita bread on picnics.

Chop the olives coarsely and combine them in a large bowl with the onions, parsley, and walnuts. Mix well. Sprinkle the mixture with pepper and Aleppo pepper and mix thoroughly. Sprinkle with lemon juice and olive oil. Garnish with pomegranate seeds, if using.

Haricot or White Bean Salad

1 cup dried cannellini or haricot beans (canned can be used)

1 teaspoon salt

5 spring onions, washed, roots removed, sliced thin with most of the greens

1 green bell pepper, seeded, ribbed, and finely chopped

½ bunch fresh Italian parsley, washed, drained, and finely chopped

DRESSING:
Juice of ½ lemon

2 teaspoons white vinegar

½ teaspoon salt

½ teaspoon sugar

¼ cup extra-virgin olive oil

GARNISH:
2 hard-cooked eggs, cut in 4 pieces lengthwise

10 black olives

SERVES 4 TO 6

This makes a great vegetarian main dish for two. If using canned beans, skip the soaking and cooking steps.

Soak the dried beans overnight and drain.

Place drained soaked beans in a medium-size pot with 3 cups of water and salt. Bring to a boil, reduce heat to medium and cook for 5 minutes, removing any scum. Cover, reduce the heat to low, and cook for 45 minutes or until tender. Drain well and let cool.

Prepare the dressing: Whisk together the lemon juice, vinegar, salt, sugar, and olive oil.

In a shallow dish place the spring onions, bell peppers, and parsley. Add the cooled or canned beans and dressing. Mix well. Decorate with eggs and olives.

Potato Puree Salad

1 pound white potatoes, washed

DRESSING:

2 tablespoons lemon juice

5 tablespoons extra-virgin olive oil

1 clove garlic, minced

$1/2$ teaspoon white vinegar

Salt

GARNISH:

2 to 3 spring onions, sliced lengthwise

6 to 7 black olives

3 hard-cooked eggs, cut in quarters, optional

10 grape tomatoes

SERVES 6

Boil potatoes in 3 cups of water for 20 to 25 minutes, covered. Cook until soft, drain, peel, and put through a ricer or mash well.

Prepare the dressing: In a small bowl, whisk together lemon juice, olive oil, garlic, vinegar, and salt to taste.

Combine the potatoes with the dressing, mixing well. Garnish with spring olives, onions, eggs, if using, and grape tomatoes.

Nur's Note: Peel the potatoes after cooking so they won't absorb so much water.

Purslane Salad

½ pound purslane (wild ones are available in Eastern and farmer's markets)

I medium onion, coarsely chopped

I large tomato, peeled and cut in ½-inch squares

½ teaspoon salt

I tablespoon fresh lemon juice

3 tablespoons extra-virgin olive oil

SERVES 4

This is a popular summer salad.

Cut off half of the thick stems of the purslane, discard any damaged leaves, and pick off the leaves by hand. Wash, drain, and gently dry with a paper towel.

Arrange the purslane in a salad bowl. Add onions, tomatoes, salt, lemon juice, and olive oil. Mix well.

Nur's Note: Another version of this salad is to prepare the pursulane (as above) and mix with Yogurt Sauce (page 43). Top with ½ teaspoon Aleppo pepper mixed with 2 teaspoons olive oil.

Salads

Red Cabbage Salad

1 head red cabbage (about 1
pound)

¼ cup red wine vinegar

3 cups boiling water

DRESSING:

2 tablespoons red wine vinegar

9 tablespoons extra-virgin
olive oil

1 tablespoon lemon juice

1 teaspoon dry mustard

1 clove garlic, minced

Salt

SERVES 4 TO 6

This is a very common winter salad in Turkey.

Remove the core of the cabbage, cut cabbage in quarters, thinly slice, and place in a large bowl.

In a small pan heat the red wine vinegar to boiling and pour over the shredded cabbage. Stir to mix well so cabbage is coated. Pour the boiling water over the cabbage and drain well.

Prepare the dressing by whisking together the vinegar, olive oil, lemon juice, mustard, garlic, and salt to taste. Pour over the cabbage and mix well. Place in a salad bowl and serve.

Shepherd's Salad

4 large tomatoes, diced in
½-inch squares

3 mild green chili peppers,
finely chopped, or 1 green
bell pepper, finely chopped

4 spring onions, finely
chopped

½ long cucumber (or 2 small
Turkish ones), peeled and
diced in ½-inch squares

10 sprigs fresh Italian parsley,
finely chopped

DRESSING:

¼ cup extra-virgin olive oil

Juice of ½ lemon

1 tablespoon white vinegar

Salt

Freshly ground pepper

GARNISH:

5 small radishes, optional

8 to 10 black olives, optional

SERVES 6

In a large salad bowl, mix together the tomatoes, chili peppers, onions, cucumbers, and parsley.

In a small bowl, beat together the olive oil, lemon juice, and vinegar. Season to taste with salt and pepper, and pour over the salad.

Partially peel the radishes, if using, in strips, and decorate the salad with radishes and black olives if desired.

Salads

Turnip Salad

1 large turnip, washed, peeled, and coarsely grated

1 ½ teaspoons salt, plus additional to taste

Juice of ½ lemon

¼ cup plus 1 tablespoon extra-virgin olive oil

GARNISH (OPTIONAL):
Carrots, cut into strips

Olives

SERVES 4

This is a winter salad.

Place the grated turnip in a large bowl, sprinkle with salt, and mix. Let sit for 15 minutes, then place turnips in a colander, wash well, and let drain. Place turnips in a serving bowl.

Mix together the lemon juice, olive oil, and salt to taste. Pour over the turnips and mix well. If desired, decorate with strips of carrots and olives.

Two Pepper Salad

1 large green bell pepper

1 large red bell pepper

1 large clove garlic

$\frac{1}{4}$ teaspoon salt

Juice of $\frac{1}{4}$ lemon

$\frac{1}{4}$ cup extra-virgin olive oil

$1\frac{1}{2}$ teaspoons balsamic
    vinegar

SERVES 2 TO 4

*P*reheat the oven to 350°F.

Bake (or grill) the bell peppers until browned and charred 10 to 15 minutes on each side. Remove them from the oven and immediately wrap them in aluminum foil (they will steam and peel easily). Let them sit for 30 minutes. Carefully peel and slice each bell pepper into 4 slices. Place on a serving platter.

Using a mortar and pestle, crush the garlic and salt together (this "marriage" makes them taste better). Place in a small bowl and add the lemon juice, olive oil, and vinegar, mixing well. Pour dressing over the bell peppers and serve.

Salads

Yogurt and Cucumber Salad

2 cucumbers (or 3 medium Turkish ones), peeled, cut in half, and seeds removed

1 pound plain natural yogurt

2 to 3 cloves garlic, minced

Salt

1 tablespoon extra-virgin olive oil

1 teaspoon dried mint

SERVES 6

This is served with rice, meat dishes, and boereks.

Grate or chop the cucumbers and place them in a colander to get rid of any excess water.

Place the yogurt in a bowl, add the garlic and salt to taste, and mix well. Add the cucumbers and mix well. Drizzle on the oil and sprinkle with the dry mint.

Poultry

Boiled Chicken

1 chicken (about 3 pounds),
washed, fat removed

1 onion

1 carrot

5 to 6 stems fresh parsley

Freshly ground pepper

1 bay leaf

SERVES 4

Boiled chicken is cooked in almost every Turkish home. In my childhood we had it once a week and used the cooking liquid to prepare a nice vermicelli soup and white rice. Whenever any of us was sick we had boiled chicken with soup since it is very light and easy to digest.

Place the chicken in a large pot with the onion, carrot, parsley, pepper, and bay leaf. Add 7 cups of water and bring to a boil. Remove any scum, cover, and reduce heat to simmer, and continue cooking for 40 to 45 minutes or until chicken is done.

Remove chicken, cool, discard any fat, and save broth for a future use.

Chicken Biryani

1 cup uncooked extra-long-grain white rice

½ teaspoon salt

1 tablespoon butter

1 small onion, finely chopped

½ Boiled Chicken (page 81), skinned, boned, and coarsely shredded

2 cups chicken stock or broth

SERVES 4

Place the rice in a bowl, cover with cold salted water, mix well and let it soak for 20 minutes. Drain well.

Preheat oven to 400°F.

Melt the butter in a pot, sauté the onion, stirring, over high heat for 3 to 4 minutes. Add the rice and cook, stirring for 3 minutes, add the chicken, stir to mix well, and cook for 2 minutes. Add the chicken stock, stir to mix well, and pour into an ovenproof casserole. Cover and bake for 12 to 15 minutes.

Remove the casserole from the oven and let it sit, covered, for 30 minutes.

Chicken Casserole

2 tablespoons vegetable oil

2 tablespoons butter

2 medium onions, finely chopped

3 cloves garlic, finely chopped

½ green bell pepper, seeded, ribbed, and diced

½ red bell pepper, seeded, ribbed, and diced

4 ounces fresh mushrooms, wiped clean and sliced

Salt

Freshly ground pepper

4 boned, skinned chicken breasts, diced in ½-inch squares

2 tomatoes, seeded and diced

1 teaspoon tomato paste

1 teaspoon Red Bell Pepper Paste (page 37)

3 medium potatoes, peeled and diced small

1 teaspoon dried thyme or oregano

SERVES 4 TO 6

*I*n a 3-quart pot heat the oil and butter. Sauté the onions, garlic, and bell peppers, stirring over medium heat for 7 minutes. Add the mushrooms, salt and pepper to taste, and cook, stirring for 2 to 3 minutes. Add the chicken and cook stirring for 5 minutes.

Add the tomatoes, tomato paste, bell pepper paste, and 3 cups water. Stir and mix well. Cover and cook for 15 minutes, stirring occasionally.

Add the potatoes and 1 to 1½ cups water, thyme or oregano. Mix well. Cover and cook, stirring occasionally, for 20 minutes.

Remove from heat and serve. It is wonderful served with rice and a green salad.

Poultry

83

Chicken Casserole With Okra

4 tablespoons vegetable oil

1 large onion, diced

4 cloves garlic, finely chopped

3 chicken thighs or 1 ½ breasts, boned, skinned, trimmed of fat, cut in ½-inch pieces

2 large tomatoes, peeled and finely chopped

Salt

Freshly ground pepper

14 ounces frozen okra, thawed and well drained

Juice of ½ lemon

SERVES 4

*I*n a 3- to 4-quart pot, heat the oil and sauté the onion and garlic, stirring, for 5 minutes. Add the chicken, stir and cook over high heat for 5 minutes. Add the tomatoes, salt and pepper to taste, continue to stir, and cook for 5 minutes. Add the okra and 1 ½ cups water. Bring to a boil reduce heat, cover, and cook over medium heat for 15 minutes.

Add the lemon juice, cover and continue cooking for 15 to 20 minutes, or until okra is tender.

Chicken, Green Beans, and Rice With Saffron

SEBZELİ TAVUKLU PİLAV

1 cup uncooked basmati rice

½ pound fresh string beans

3 tablespoons vegetable oil

2 boned, skinned chicken breasts cut into 1-inch cubes

Salt

Freshly ground pepper

1 onion, chopped

1 large tomato, peeled and diced

Pinch of saffron mixed with 1 tablespoon water

1 tablespoon butter

MAKES 4 LARGE OR 6 SMALL SERVINGS

Soak the rice in enough water to cover for 20 minutes. Trim the ends of the beans and cut beans into 1-inch pieces.

Heat the oil in 3-quart pot and sauté the chicken over medium heat, stirring for 3 to 4 minutes. Add salt and pepper to taste, mix well, and remove the chicken from the pot, place on a plate, cover, and set aside.

Add the onions and beans to the pot, turn heat to high, and cook stirring for 10 minutes. Reduce heat, add the tomatoes, and cook, stirring for 5 minutes. Return the chicken to the pot, add 2 cups of water, and mix well. Turn the heat to high and adjust the seasoning.

Drain the rice and add to the pot along with the saffron and water mixture and the butter. Bring to a boil, reduce heat to low, cover, and cook for 10 minutes.

Remove pot from the heat, uncover, place a sheet of paper towel over the top of the pot, and replace the lid. Set aside for 5 to 7 minutes.

Using the back of a wooden spoon, mix everything and place in a serving bowl.

Chicken Shish Kebab

8 chicken thighs, boned, skinned and fat removed

1 onion, grated

2 green bell peppers, ribbed, seeded, and cut into 1-inch pieces

2 red bell peppers, ribbed, seeded, and cut into 1-inch pieces

3 onions, cut into 1-inch pieces

1 or 2 long hot green chili peppers, cut into ½-inch pieces, optional

MARINADE:

8 tablespoons yogurt

4 tablespoons soy sauce

Juice of 1 lemon

3 tablespoons chopped fresh Italian parsley

1 teaspoon fresh oregano

4 tablespoons vegetable oil

6 to 8 cloves garlic, minced

SERVES 4

Slice each thigh in half horizontally. Place them on a wooden board and pound them with a meat tenderizer until flat and even in width. Cut each piece in half so you have 2 long pieces. Carefully roll up each piece, using any small pieces if needed to make the roll. Squeeze the grated onion over the chicken.

Thread the chicken on the skewers, each skewer should have 4 or 5 rolls, alternating the chicken with the green and red bell peppers, onion chunks, and chili pepper, if desired.

Combine the yogurt, soy sauce, lemon juice, parsley, oregano, oil, and garlic. Mix well. Place the threaded skewers in the marinade and coat all sides of the chicken rolls. Let chicken sit in the marinade for at least 1 hour.

Heat the grill or broiler. Cook the chicken for 10 minutes, turning onto all 4 sides to cook. Remove from heat and serve.

Chicken With Vegetables in a Clay Pot

I large Asian eggplant

Salt

Freshly ground pepper

5 cloves garlic, sliced

3 tablespoons vegetable oil

8 chicken legs (drumsticks)
   or 2 boned breasts cut into
   $1/2$-inch pieces

$1/2$ pound fresh okra

$1/2$ pound string beans

I tablespoon butter

2 large onions, finely chopped

3 large tomatoes, coarsely
   chopped

2 large green bell peppers,
   seeded, ribbed, and cut in
   chunks

I teaspoon Red Bell Pepper
   Paste (page 37)

3 medium potatoes, peeled,
   and cut in chunks

3 zucchini, sliced in $1/2$-inch
   pieces, then sliced in half

SERVES 6

Clay pots are common pieces of cooking equipment in Turkish kitchens, and are used over very very low heat on the burners or in the oven. You can use a metal pot.

Cut eggplant in 2-inch chunks, salt, and let sit in a colander over a bowl for 30 minutes, then rinse well and pat dry.

Combine the salt and pepper to taste, garlic and oil in a bowl and marinate the chicken for 30 minutes.

With a sharp knife, peel the okra in a circular clockwise motion, beginning at the stem and coming down about $1/3$-inch. Cut the tips from the string beans, and cut each bean in half or in pieces 2 inches long.

Preheat the oven to 400°F.

In a pot, melt the butter and add the chicken and sauté. Stir, cooking over medium heat for 5 minutes, turning chicken pieces once.

In a separate bowl, mix onions, tomatoes, beans, bell peppers. Sprinkle the top of the chicken with $1/4$ of the onion mixture along with and a little salt and pepper. Repeat with another layer of $1/4$ of the onion, salt and pepper. Add bell pepper paste, cover and cook on low heat for 20 minutes.

Poultry

87

Continued

Uncover and make a layer of all the potatoes. Top with ¼ of the remaining onion mixture, salt, and pepper. Top with a layer of eggplant chunks, then more onion mixture, salt, and pepper. Top with a layer of zucchini, ¼ more onion mixture, salt, and pepper.

Add a layer of okra. Finish with the remaining onion mixture, salt, and pepper. Pour ½ cup water over the top, cover and bake for 55 to 60 minutes. Uncover the casserole and bake another 5 minutes.

Chicken With Walnuts

3- to 4-pound chicken

1 onion, peeled and kept whole

1 bay leaf

1 carrot, peeled and kept whole

4 to 5 peppercorns

½ teaspoon salt

SAUCE:

3 slices stale bread

1 ½ cup ground walnuts

1 clove garlic, chopped

1 cup chicken stock

½ cup milk

TOPPING:

1 tablespoon vegetable oil

1 teaspoon paprika

SERVES 6 TO 8

This dish can be served as a starter or is an ideal dish for a buffet. It is best when prepared one day ahead. It is not suitable for freezing.

Wash and clean the chicken and make sure no giblets are left inside. Place the chicken in a large pot, cover with cold water, add the onion, bay leaf, carrot, peppercorns, and salt. Bring to boil, reduce heat to medium and cook for 45 to 60 minutes or until chicken is done. If any scum appears remove it with a slotted spoon. When done, remove the chicken from the pot and save the cooking liquid.

After the chicken has cooled, remove the skin, bones, and any fat. Shred the chicken into pieces 1 ½ inches long by ½ inch wide. Arrange the chicken pieces in a shallow serving dish.

Place the stale bread, ground walnuts, chopped garlic, chicken stock, and milk in a large bowl. Mix well with a wooden spoon, then place mixture in a blender and puree. Add sauce to the shredded chicken and mix well.

In a small bowl place the oil and paprika. Mix well and drizzle it over the chicken making round or oval patterns.

Zucchini Boats With Chicken

5 to 6 large Turkish zucchini

1 teaspoon salt

1 leg and thigh from a 4-pound Boiled Chicken (page 81) (or 2 legs and thighs from a 2- to 3-pound chickens)

2 tablespoons butter

2 tablespoons all-purpose flour

1 cup milk

1 bay leaf

Freshly ground pepper

3/4 cup grated white cheddar or Gouda cheese

SERVES 6 AS A MAIN COURSE, OR 12 AS A STARTER

Turkish zucchini are available at farmer's markets. They are pale green, 6 inches long, and ideal for stuffing.

Trim the stems and tips from the zucchini and scrape off the peel (the scraper edge of a vegetable corer gives a beautiful striped effect). Cut the zucchini in half lengthwise.

In a large pot place 6 cups of water and 1 teaspoon of salt. Bring to a boil and add the zucchini halves. Cover the pot, bring to a boil, and cook for 5 to 7 minutes (zucchini should not be too soft or mushy). Drain well in a colander.

Shred the chicken, removing all pieces of fat, skin, bones, and any discolored pieces. Place the chicken in a large bowl.

In a 2-quart pot melt the butter, remove pot from the heat, and quickly whisk in the flour. Return the pot to the heat and continue whisking over low heat. Add the milk and bay leaf. Cook, whisking over low heat, until sauce thickens. Add salt and pepper to taste, discard the bay leaf, and add 1/4 cup of the cheese. Mix the sauce with the chicken.

Preheat oven to 400°F.

Scoop out the zucchini leaving only a 1/2-inch shell. Place the zucchini shells in a 9 by 13-inch baking dish, greased with butter. Fill the shells with the chicken mixture and top with the remaining 1/2 cup cheese. Bake for 5 minutes and place the pan under the broiler until the tops are golden brown. Watch the zucchini carefully so they do not burn.

Turkey With Prunes

1 12- to 13-pound turkey

1 tablespoon salt

2 tablespoons mustard

½ to 1 cup vegetable oil

1 large onion, finely chopped

1 large fennel, coarsely chopped

3 oranges with skin, each cut in 8 pieces

24 ounces pitted dried prunes

SERVES 10 TO 12

This is from a Dutch friend, Geert Veentjer. His mother used to make it. While he was spending a New Year's holiday with us, we made this recipe to commemorate his mother and all loved it. It became our New Year's Eve favorite.

Wash the turkey, rub with salt and mustard, and let rest for 1 hour at room temperature.

In a large skillet, heat the oil and sauté turkey until each side is golden brown. Place the turkey in a large turkey roaster, add onion, fennel, oranges, prunes, and add 8 cups of water.

Bring to a boil, reduce heat to medium, and cook, covered, for 2 hours. After 30 minutes, baste the turkey every 15 to 20 minutes with the cooking liquid. When turkey is done, set it aside, discard the oranges, and place the prunes on a plate (to serve later). Carve the turkey, arrange the prunes around the meat and serve. The juice becomes a tasty gravy.

Fish and Seafood

Codfish Steaks in Clay Pot

3 tablespoons extra-virgin olive oil

4 codfish steaks

4 potatoes, peeled and cut into chunks

3 long green chili peppers or cubanel peppers, seeded, ribbed, and cut in 2-inch pieces

Salt

Freshly ground pepper

1 cup pureed canned tomatoes

1/2 teaspoon oregano

SERVES 4

Preheat oven to 400°F.

Place the oil in the bottom of the clay pot or casserole and rub fish around in the oil on both sides. Place the potatoes on top the fish and then the peppers. Sprinkle with salt and pepper to taste and pour the pureed tomatoes over everything.

Add 1/2 cup water, and sprinkle with oregano. Cover and bake for 30 to 35 minutes or until fish and potatoes are done. Remove from oven and let rest, covered for 5 to 10 minutes, then serve.

Fried Mussels

MİDYE TAVA

2 pounds frozen green New
Zealand half shell mussels
(about 36)

1 cup all-purpose flour

1 teaspoon salt

½ teaspoon baking soda

Vegetable oil for frying

Tarator Sauce (page 106)

SERVES 6

This is a recipe prepared by the street vendors in Istanbul.

Remove the mussels from the shells and discard the shells. Arrange 4 or 5 mussels on a bamboo skewer leaving a little space in between each one.

In a bowl mix together the flour and salt. In a large bowl mix together 2 cups of water and the baking soda.

Heat enough oil to cover the bottom of a large frying pan to a depth of ¼ to ½ inch (oil must be very hot).

Flour the mussels by holding the ends of the skewers and dipping them on both sides. After the mussels have been dipped in the flour, quickly dip them into the water mixture (be sure the baking soda is dissolved in the water and not sitting on the bottom of the bowl... you may need to stir before each skewer is dipped). Carefully and quickly place the skewers in the hot oil (the water may cause the oil to shoot up so stand away from the skillet). Fry the mussels, turning once, for 2 minutes. Do not overcook them. Drain well on paper towel and serve with Tarator Sauce.

Fried Turbot

3 pounds turbot fillets

I tablespoon salt

I cup all-purpose flour

I cup vegetable oil for frying

GARNISH:
Lemon quarters

SERVES 4 TO 5

Turbot is considered the king of the fish in Turkey. Usually you start eating with your fork and knife and end up eating with your hands!

Wash the turbot and gently pat dry. Sprinkle the fish with salt and dip in flour. Shake each piece to get rid of excess flour.

Heat the oil in a large frying pan and fry over medium heat until golden brown on both sides, turning once or twice. Arrange a few layers of paper towels and drain the fried fish to get rid of any excess oil. Serve with lemon quarters and Arugula Salad (page 63) topped with rings of fresh Spanish onions.

Fish and Seafood

Gray Mullet Pilaki

¼ cup extra-virgin olive oil

2 onions, finely chopped

2 medium carrots, diced

1 stalk celery, thinly sliced

2 garlic cloves, finely
chopped

2 medium potatoes, peeled
and diced

Salt

2 tomatoes, peeled and finely
chopped

2 pounds gray mullet, sliced
crosswise into ½-inch-
thick pieces (or 4 tuna
steaks)

GARNISH:

2 tablespoon finely chopped
fresh Italian parsley

1 lemon, cut in quarters
lengthwise

SERVES 4

Fish "pilaki" dishes are one of the main stays of Turkish dishes. These are done by first sautéing the vegetables, adding the fish, gently cooking it, and eating it at room temperature. Pilaki always includes onions, garlic, celery, carrot, and potatoes cooked in olive oil. Haricot beans, cranberry beans, and mussels can be done the same way.

In a large skillet, heat the oil and sauté the onions, carrots, celery, and garlic over medium heat for 6 to 7 minutes, stirring constantly. Then add potatoes, salt, and tomatoes. Cook, stirring, for 4 minutes. Add 1 cup of water, cover, and cook for 8 to 10 minutes.

Place the fish in a sauté pan and pour the vegetable mixture over the fish. Cover and cook on low heat 20 minutes or until fish flakes easily with a fork. Remove pan from the heat. Remove the lid and add the chopped parsley. Partially cover and let cool to room temperature.

Serve with a green salad, lemon quarters, and warm country bread.

Marinated Shrimp on Skewers

⅓ cup extra-virgin olive oil

4 to 5 cloves garlic, minced

1 pound fresh shrimp, peeled

GARNISH:
Lemon wedges

MAKES APPROXIMATELY 6 SKEWERS

*I*n a large bowl combine the olive oil and garlic, mixing well. Add the shrimp and mix well to coat each one with marinade. Cover and refrigerate overnight.

Place 5 shrimp on each wooden skewer. Over medium heat, heat a griddle or skillet. Lay the shrimp on the griddle or skillet and cook turning once or twice. Do not overcook the shrimp—1½ to 2 minutes per side should suffice.

Serve with lemon wedges.

Fish and Seafood

Mussel Pilaki

36 large mussels in the shell or 2 pounds frozen green New Zealand mussels on the half shell, thawed

½ cup extra-virgin olive oil

2 onions, finely chopped

5 cloves garlic, finely chopped

2 medium carrots, sliced crosswise into ½-inch-thick pieces

1 large potato, peeled and diced into ½-inch squares

2 celery stalks, sliced thin

2 tomatoes, peeled and finely chopped

1 teaspoon sugar

1 teaspoon salt

2 tablespoons finely chopped fresh parsley

SERVES 6

If using fresh mussels: wash the mussels under running water and scrub them with a brush. Discard any open mussels. Open them carefully, cut off the beards, and gently remove the meat. Wash the mussels, drain well, and discard the shells. Boil a quart of water, add the mussels, and cook them for 3 to 4 minutes. Remove them using a slotted spoon, set them aside, and save 1 cup of the cooking liquid.

If using frozen thawed mussels: carefully remove (cut) the mussel from the shell and discard the shells. Do not boil these mussels.

In a large sauté pan heat the oil and sauté the onions, stirring, for 5 to 8 minutes over medium heat. Add the garlic and carrots and cook another 2 to 3 minutes, stirring. Add the potato, celery, tomatoes, sugar, and salt, mixing well and cooking for 2 minutes. Stir in the reserved cooking liquid from the fresh mussels or 1 cup water for the frozen ones and ½ cup of warm water. Cook, covered over low medium heat until all the vegetables are done, about 30 minutes. Most of the water will have been absorbed but if more is needed you can add another ¼ cup of warm water.

Add the mussels, mixing well, and cook, covered, for 2 to 3 minutes. Remove the pan from the heat and sprinkle the parsley over the top. Eat at room temperature.

Mussels Stuffed With Rice

1 cup uncooked long-grain white rice

4 teaspoons salt

¾ cup extra-virgin olive oil

1 pound onions, finely chopped

3 tablespoons pine nuts

1 large tomato, peeled and finely chopped

3 tablespoons currants, washed

2 teaspoons sugar

½ teaspoon pepper

1 cup boiling water

40 large mussels in the shells

1 large onion, sliced

1 large lemon, peeled and sliced crosswise

SERVES 6 TO 8

This can also be used as an appetizer.

Soak rice in 3 cups of water mixed with 1 teaspoon salt for 20 minutes and drain well.

In a pan heat ½ cup olive oil, add onions and sauté for 8 to 10 minutes on medium heat, constantly stirring. Add the drained rice and pine nuts and sauté them for 5 to 6 minutes, stirring. Add tomatoes, stir for a couple of minutes more, then add currants, 2 teaspoons salt, 1 teaspoon sugar, and the pepper. Add boiling water, cover, and simmer until all the water is absorbed. Set aside to cool. While rice is cooling you can prepare the mussels for stuffing.

Clean the mussels with a wire brush under running water. Let them soak in water for 30 minutes. Carefully open each shell on the flat side (opposite the side where the shell is attached) with the back of a knife. Try not to pull the two sections apart. Cut the hairy beard off, wash, and drain well. Each mussel will be stuffed with a teaspoon of rice stuffing and closed tightly. (If your mussels are not large you need to put less stuffing to close it tightly).

Put the sliced onions on the bottom of a 4-quart pot (covering the bottom completely). Place the mussels side by side, make a second layer on top of the first, and cover mussels with lemon slices. Add 1 teaspoon salt, 1 teaspoon sugar, ¼ cup olive oil, and 2 cups of water.

Fish and Seafood

Continued

Cover the top with a circle of parchment paper, place a plate upside down on the top the parchment to weigh down the mussels, and cover the pot. This way there is no chance for the mussels to open. Bring to a boil, reduce heat, then simmer 35 to 40 minutes. Let them cool in the pot. Remove plate and paper and serve warm, room temperature, or chilled. They can be eaten the next day.

Stuffed mussels are eaten with a teaspoon by scooping out the mussel and stuffing. Serve with Arugula Salad (page 63).

Red Snapper

All-purpose flour

Salt

1 pound red snapper (2 fillets)

½ cup vegetable oil

GARNISH:

Lemon wedges

SERVES 2

Combine the flour and salt. Dip the fish in the flour mixture, coating both sides.

Heat the oil in a skillet large enough to hold the fish. Add the fish and cook for 3 minutes per side, turning once. Cook until the fish flakes easily with a fork.

Drain well on paper towels and serve with Onion Relish (page 115) and lemon wedges.

Salmon in Parchment Paper Packages

4 teaspoons butter, softened to room temperature

1 large lemon, peel removed and sliced into 8 thin slices

1 (2-pound) salmon fillet, skin removed, cut in 4 pieces

1 large tomato, peeled and sliced into 8 thin slices

½ green bell pepper, seeded, ribbed, and cut into small strips

4 ounces fresh mushrooms, wiped clean and sliced thin

2 tablespoons finely chopped Italian (flat leaf) parsley

Salt

Freshly ground pepper

SERVES 4

A very elegant main course.

Cut 4 parchment paper ovals 14 by 10 ½ inches. Butter each oval on one side. Position oval so short edge is closest to you. Place 2 slices of lemon in the bottom half of each oval and place a piece of salmon on the lemons. Place 2 slices of tomato on each piece of salmon and some bell pepper strips. Then place 2 or 3 slices of mushrooms and top with chopped parsley. Sprinkle with salt and pepper to taste.

Preheat oven to 375°F.

Fold the parchment in half over the fish so the straight edge is on top and the rounded edge on the bottom facing you. Fold a small triangle from the top right corner over onto the parchment and continue folding triangles as you work your way around the parchment. As you fold each narrow triangle it will enclose the previous triangle. The parchment will almost look as if it had been crimped. When you reach the top left corner, fold the triangle over and tuck it into the preceding triangle to seal. Repeat folding and sealing the remaining packages. Place the packages on an ungreased cookie sheet and sprinkle the tops of the packages with water. Press to remove air. This will keep them from burning in the oven.

Bake for 20 minutes. Using a scissors, cut a semicircle around the top of the package 1 inch in from the outer edge to expose the salmon. Bend the cut piece back toward the straight edge and serve.

Sardines Wrapped in Grape Leaves

ASMA YAPRAĞINDA SARDALYA

½ cup extra-virgin olive oil

Juice of 1½ lemons

1 teaspoon salt

¼ teaspoon white pepper

30 fresh sardines

30 grape leaves (fresh or
from a jar)

GARNISH:
2 lemons, quartered

SERVES 6

The leaves protect the delicate fish from burning and provide additional flavor.

Prepare the marinade by mixing the olive oil, lemon juice, salt, and pepper. Without removing the heads and tails of the sardines, carefully remove the backbones and scrape off the scales. Place sardines in the marinade, and let sit for 30 minutes.

If using fresh leaves, boil for 1 minute and then drain well. If using leaves from a jar, soak them for 20 minutes in warm water to remove excess salt, then drain well. Open each grape leaf and place shiny side down rib side up on a work surface.

Lay a fish on each leaf and roll up leaving the head and tails sticking out. Brush the rolled leaves all over with olive oil and grill about 4 to 5 minutes on each side Unwrap the leaves, discard the leaves, and enjoy the delicious taste of the sardines. Serve with lemon quarters.

Sautéed Squid With Tarator Sauce

TARATOR SOSLU SOTE KALAMAR

MARINADE:

4 tablespoons white wine

4 tablespoons extra-virgin olive oil

1 pound squid, washed (do not remove tentacles)

TARATOR SAUCE:

2 thick slices white bread, crusts removed

3 cloves garlic, finely minced

1/2 teaspoon salt

1/2 cup finely ground walnuts

2/3 cup extra-virgin olive oil

Juice of 1 lemon

1/4 cup extra-virgin olive oil for frying

SERVES 3 TO 4 WITH 1 CUP SAUCE

In a bowl combine the wine and olive oil. Place the squid in the marinade and coat both sides of the pieces. Let squid rest in this marinade for at least 5 to 6 hours (or even for a day) before grilling.

Cut large squid pieces in half. With a sharp knife make parallel lines about 1/2 inch wide across the squid. Turn the pieces the other way and repeat making parallel lines. This lets the squid curl.

Prepare the sauce. Soak the bread in water for a couple of minutes, squeeze dry, and crumble. Place the bread, garlic, salt, walnuts, olive oil, and lemon juice in a blender and blend until smooth.

In a large skillet, heat the olive oil, and add the squid. Cook 3 to 4 minutes turning once or twice, drain well and serve with sauce.

Nur's Note: The Tarator Sauce can be served with fried, grilled squid or fried mussels.

Shrimp Casserole

8 tablespoons butter

2 pounds shrimp, peeled

3 cloves garlic, minced

1 green pepper, ribbed, seeded, and chopped

1 red pepper, ribbed, seeded, and chopped

8 ounces fresh mushrooms, wiped clean and sliced in half

1 ½ pounds tomatoes, peeled and seeded

1 cup dry white wine

1 teaspoon dried oregano

1 bay leaf

Salt

Freshly ground pepper

1 tablespoon all-purpose flour

SERVES 8

If you are using frozen or precooked shrimp, do not cook them in the butter, just add them to the sauce after the flour and water mixture has been added.

Melt 4 tablespoons of butter in a large skillet over medium heat. When the butter is hot, sauté the shrimp, stirring, for 3 to 4 minutes. Remove them from the skillet and set aside.

Add 4 tablespoons of butter to the skillet and sauté the garlic, green pepper, and red pepper, stirring, for 5 minutes. Add the mushrooms and cook another 2 minutes. Add the tomatoes, ¼ to ½ cup water (depending on how juicy the tomatoes are), wine, oregano, bay leaf, salt and pepper to taste, and continue cooking until mixture begins to boil. Stir to mix well. Remove the bay leaf and discard.

In a small bowl mix the flour into 1 tablespoon water and add the mixture to the simmering sauce, stirring or whisking to blend well. Return the shrimp to the pan and continue to cook, simmering for 10 minutes. Remove pan and serve shrimp over rice.

Fish and Seafood

Steamed Sea Bass

2 tablespoons butter

2 medium onions, halved
and sliced into thin semicircles

1/4 cup all-purpose flour

2 pounds sea bass fillets, cut
into 10 to 12 equal pieces

6 ounces fresh button mushrooms, washed and stems
trimmed

2 bay leaves

1 lemon, peeled and sliced
crosswise

1/2 teaspoon salt

5 to 6 black peppercorns

5 to 6 fresh stems Italian
parsley, tied in a bunch

1/2 cup white wine

1/4 cup whipping cream

SERVES 6

Dot the bottom of a large sauté pan with butter and arrange the slices of 1 of the onions on top of the butter. Flour both sides of the fish pieces and shake to remove any excess flour. Place the fish side by side on top of the onions, then add the rest of the onions, mushrooms, bay leaves, lemon slices, salt, peppercorns, and parsley stems over the fish. Add 1/2 cup of water and the wine and bring to a boil. Reduce heat, cover, and simmer for 15 minutes. Add the cream, simmer 2 to 3 minutes more, and remove from the heat.

Carefully place the fish on a serving dish. Discard the lemon slices, bay leaves, and parsley stems. Serve with boiled red potatoes and a green salad.

Stuffed Mackerel

1 fresh mackerel, cleaned

2 spring onions, sliced thin

¼ cup chopped fresh Italian
   parsley

Salt

Freshly ground pepper

Vegetable oil

SERVES 2

*P*reheat oven to 400°F.

Lightly oil a baking dish and place the fish in
it. Combine the onions and parsley and stuff
inside the fish. Sprinkle fish with salt and
freshly ground pepper to taste, and lightly oil
the top part of the fish. Bake for 25 minutes
or until done.

Fish and Seafood

Swordfish Shish Kebab

MARINADE:

¼ cup extra-virgin olive oil

Juice of 1 lemon

Salt

Freshly ground pepper

1 teaspoon lemon pepper
    seasoning

1 pound swordfish, cut into
    2-inch cubes

Bay leaves

1 lemon, sliced thin

1 small tomato, cut into
    ¼-inch slices

1 red or green bell pepper,
    seeded, ribs removed, and
    cut into 1-inch squares

SERVES 4

In a bowl combine the olive oil, lemon juice, salt and pepper to taste, and lemon pepper. Thread the fish on skewers alternating with bay leaves, lemon slices, tomato slices, and bell peppers. Place skewers in a shallow dish and let fish marinate, covered, in the refrigerator until ready to use.

Preheat oven to broil, or heat up your grill when you are ready to cook. Cook 5 to 7 minutes on each side. Do not overcook.

Whiting

2 fillets (1 pound) whiting,
   cut in half

All-purpose flour

½ cup vegetable oil for frying

GARNISH:
1 lemon, cut into wedges

SERVES 2

*D*ip the pieces of fish in the flour, coating both sides.

Heat the oil in a large skillet that will hold all the pieces of fish. Place the fish in the hot oil and cook on each side until fish flakes easily with a fork. Drain well on paper towels and serve with Onion Relish (page 115) if desired, and lemon wedges.

Whiting Patties

I pound whiting fillets

I bay leaf

I onion, finely chopped

3 slices white bread, crusts removed, soaked in water, squeezed dry

2 tablespoons finely chopped fresh Italian parsley

¼ teaspoon salt

¼ teaspoon white pepper

¼ teaspoon cumin

¼ teaspoon Aleppo pepper

I egg yolk

½ cup all-purpose flour

½ cup vegetable oil for frying

GARNISH:

Lemon wedges

Spring onions

SERVES 4 AS A MAIN COURSE,
6 AS A STARTER

Arrange fish fillets in a pan, cover with ¾ cup of water and the I bay leaf, and bring to a boil. Reduce heat, cover, and simmer for 5 minutes. Remove from heat and let fish cool. Drain and shred the fish, checking carefully to remove all the bones.

Place the shredded fish in a bowl, add onion, bread, parsley, salt, white pepper, cumin, Aleppo pepper, and egg yolk, and using your fingers, mix and knead well. Divide the mixture into 12 balls, flatten and flour each patty.

In a large skillet, heat the oil and fry the patties for 2 to 3 minutes per side. Serve with lemon wedges, Arugula Salad (page 63), and spring onions.

Beef and Lamb

Albanian Liver With Onion Relish

ONION RELISH:

1 Spanish onion cut in quarters and sliced thin

Salt

1 cup chopped fresh Italian parsley

1 teaspoon sumac (available in Middle Eastern markets)

LIVER:

½ cup all-purpose flour

1 pound lamb or calf's liver (with all membrane removed), cut into pieces 1- by ½-inch

1 teaspoon Aleppo pepper

¼ cup vegetable oil

SERVES 4

The onion relish can also be used with any grilled or fried fish recipe.

Place the onion in a bowl and sprinkle with a little salt. Let it sit for 10 minutes. Rinse the salt off, drain the onion well, and let dry on paper towels. Combine the onion, parsley, and sumac, mixing well. Set aside or chill.

Place the flour in a bowl and coat the liver. Sprinkle Aleppo pepper over the liver. Heat the oil in a skillet and add the liver. Cook over high heat, stirring, for 2 to 3 minutes or until the liver is done. Do not overcook the liver.

Place the liver on a serving platter and serve with the onion relish.

Beef and Lamb

Baked Lamb Shanks à la Tandour

1 large onion, coarsely
   chopped
2 carrots, sliced
2 cloves garlic, sliced
3 bay leaves
4 lamb shanks with meat
Freshly ground pepper
½ cup boiling water

SERVES 4

*P*reheat oven to 400°F.

In the bottom of an ovenproof casserole place the onion, carrots, garlic, and bay leaves. Place the lamb on top of the vegetables and stuff a few slices of the garlic into the lamb, grind some pepper on top. Add the boiling water, cover the pot with a piece of aluminum foil and then cover with the lid.

Bake for 30 minutes, reduce heat to 350°F, and continue baking for 2 hours. Before serving, remove any fat and bones.

Boiled Lamb With Vegetables and Lemon Sauce

SEBZELİ TERBİYELİ KUZU HAŞLAMA

2 tablespoons vegetable oil

4 lamb shanks with meat

7½ cups boiling water

2 shallots

2 bay leaves

2 carrots, cut into 1-inch chunks

4 potatoes, peeled and cut into small chunks

LEMON SAUCE:

2 egg yolks

Juice of 1 lemon

1 tablespoon all-purpose flour

½ cup plain yogurt

1 tablespoon Drained Yogurt (page 42)

SERVES 4

In a large pot, heat the oil and sear the lamb shanks, turning and cooking until outer meat has changed color. Add 6 cups of boiling water, the shallots, and bay leaves. Bring to a boil, reduce heat to medium, cover and continue cooking for 1 hour and 20 minutes.

Add another 1½ cups of boiling water and the carrots and potatoes. Continue to cook, Covered, for another 20 to 25 minutes or until vegetables and meat are tender.

Meanwhile prepare the lemon sauce. In a bowl whisk together 1 cup water, egg yolks, lemon juice, flour, yogurt, and drained yogurt. Whisk to mix well. Whisk in ½ cup of the boiling liquid from the skillet, whisking constantly. When blended, add sauce to the skillet, whisk and cook for a couple of minutes. Remove skillet from the heat. Serve sauce with the lamb and vegetables.

Dried Baby Okra With Lamb

KUZU ETLİ KURU BAMYA

½ pound dried baby okra, washed well

3 tablespoons butter

1 tablespoon vegetable oil

1½ pounds lamb (leg), in 1-inch cubes

1 large onion, finely chopped

1 (14.5-ounce) can chopped tomatoes with its juice

Salt

Freshly ground pepper

Juice of ½ lemon

SERVES 6

Sun drying vegetables is an old Turkish tradition. They were eaten during long cold winter months. Still it is done in the eastern part of Turkey and Anatolia and dried vegetables are available in the markets in the big cities. When I found dried baby okra imported from Turkey in the market in Virginia, I couldn't resist adding this recipe to our book.

Boil 4 cups of water in a pot and add the dried okra. Boil for 3 to 4 minutes, uncovered, remove from the heat, cover, and let sit for 3 hours. Drain okra.

In a large pan heat butter and vegetable oil on high heat and sauté the lamb for 5 to 6 minutes. Add the onions and continue stirring another 5 minutes. Add tomatoes and cook 2 to 3 minutes. Add 1½ cups of water, cover, and let cook about 50 minutes over medium heat. Add the drained okra and check the water. If the lamb has absorbed all the water you can add 1½ cups hot water along with the okra. Since the okra is dried it needs more water than fresh ones. Add salt and pepper to taste and mix well. Cook over medium heat 40 to 45 minutes. Five minutes before the cooking has finished, add the lemon juice. Serve hot with rice.

Eggplant Kebabs From Kazan

KAZAN KEBABI

4 long narrow light purple
   Chinese eggplants or
   6 Italian eggplants

1 pound ground beef

1 medium onion, grated

Salt

4 tomatoes, peeled and finely
   chopped

2 long green chili peppers,
   seed, ribbed, and sliced

2 tablespoons butter, softened to room temperature

SERVES 4 TO 6

Trim the stems and tips from the eggplants, slice them crosswise into 1-inch slices, and leave them in the shape of the whole eggplant.

In a bowl combine the meat, grated onion, and salt to taste, mixing well. Place a walnut-size piece of meat in your hands and roll into a small ball. Place the ball between the first 2 slices of eggplant and press the 2 slices and meat together with your fingers. Continue until all the slices of 1 eggplant have a meatball between them. Carefully press the ends and pieces together so the eggplant is reassembled with the meat between the slices. Pressing firmly, lift and place the eggplant/meatball kebab into a large skillet or sauté pan. Repeat using the remaining eggplants and meat.

Sprinkle the kebabs with the tomatoes and strips of pepper. Pour a cup of water around the kebabs and dot the top of the kebabs with butter. Bring the water to a boil, reduce heat to simmer, cover, and cook for 25 minutes. Serve with rice.

Beef and Lamb

119

Eggplant Moussaka

6 Italian eggplants

Salt

1 cup plus 3 tablespoons
   vegetable oil for frying

1 large onion, diced

½ pound ground meat

3 large tomatoes, peeled and
   coarsely chopped

Freshly ground pepper

SERVES 4 TO 6

Remove the stems of the eggplant. Peel eggplant skins vertically in ½-inch strips from top to bottom at intervals for a striped effect (leaving one strip with peel and one without). Slice them crosswise in ½ inch-thick slices. Sprinkle slices with salt and place in a colander. Let sit 30 minutes then wash eggplants and pat dry with paper towels.

In a large skillet, heat ½ cup of he oil and fry eggplants (2 minutes on each side). Remove eggplants and place them on paper towels to drain.

In a sauce pan heat 3 tablespoons of the vegetable oil, add the onions, and sauté for 3 to 4 minutes, stirring. Add the meat, sauté for 6 to7 minutes, add tomatoes, salt and pepper to taste, and cook for 4 to 5 minutes.

In a sauté pan, arrange 1 layer of eggplant, cover with half the meat, make another layer of eggplant, and finish with another layer of meat. Add 1 cup of water and cook 15 to 20 minutes on medium heat. Serve with salad and rice.

Eggplant Stuffed With Meat

6 Italian eggplants, 6 to 8 inches long

Salt

Vegetable oil for frying

2 tablespoons olive oil

2 or 3 small or medium onions, finely chopped

1 green bell pepper, seeded, ribs removed, and chopped fine

1 pound ground beef

1 tomato, peeled, cut in half, and sliced thin

1 green bell pepper, seeded, ribs removed, and sliced in $1/2$-inch pieces

$1/2$ cup chopped fresh Italian parsley

$1 1/2$ cups tomato sauce

SERVES 6

Remove the leaves around the stem of the eggplant, leaving the stem on. Leave 1½-inch rim of peel around the top and bottom of the eggplant and remove the peel from the rest of the eggplant. Cut a thin slice from the bottom of the eggplant so it is flat. With a sharp knife make a vertical slit from the top of the peeled area to the bottom of the peeled area completely through the eggplant. Repeat on all eggplants. Place the eggplants on a large platter and sprinkle with salt. Let the eggplants sit with the salt for 20 to 30 minutes, rinse well, and gently dry on a kitchen towel.

Place 2 to 3 inches of vegetable oil in a 5- or 6-quart pot and heat on high heat for 10 minutes. Cook 2 to 4 eggplants at a time, depending on the size of the pot. Roll them frequently so they will lightly brown on all sides and cook evenly. Remove the eggplants from the oil when they are soft and let them drain in a fine sieve or colander. Cook remaining eggplants the same way. Place the cooked eggplants in one or two large ovenproof skillets with the cut side up. Using a spoon carefully open the slit to widen it in the middle.

In a large skillet heat the 2 tablespoons olive oil and sauté the onions and bell pepper. Cook, stirring for 5 minutes, then add the beef and stir using the side of a wooden spoon to break the meat into small pieces. Add salt to taste and continue cooking until the meat is done and no pink shows. Drain the meat to remove any excess liquid.

Beef and Lamb

Preheat the oven to 400°F.

Stuff the meat carefully into the eggplants with a spoon, pressing gently on the filling. Stuff each eggplant while it is hot. Garnish each with a slice of tomato and a strip of green pepper. Sprinkle with fresh parsley.

Pour the tomato sauce around the sides of the eggplant. Do not get any on the eggplants. Cover the pan(s) and cook over medium heat. Bring to a boil and cook 5 minutes. Remove from the heat and remove the cover from the pan(s).

Place uncovered in the oven and cook for 30 minutes. Remove the pan(s) from the oven and let cool to room temperature until serving.

Serve with rice and salad.

Forest Lamb

2 tablespoons butter

1 tablespoon vegetable oil

1 large onion, chopped

1 pound lamb (leg), cut in
¾-inch cubes

1 teaspoon all-purpose flour

10 ounces fresh button
mushrooms, wiped clean,
and stems trimmed

½ cup frozen peas

1 teaspoon finely chopped
fresh thyme

SERVES 4

Our chef, Ali Tonbul comes from Bolu. This is a specialty of his hometown.

Over high heat in a 3-quart pot, heat the butter and oil, sauté the onions, stir and cook for 5 minutes. Add the lamb, mix well, and continue to cook, stirring for 5 minutes. Add the flour and 2 cups of water, mix well, and cook for 2 minutes. Cover the pan and bring the liquid to a boil, boil for a minute or two, reduce heat to simmer, and cook for 35 minutes.

Add the mushrooms and peas, mixing well. Continue to simmer, covered, for another 20 to 25 minutes. Remove the pot from the heat and sprinkle lamb with thyme and serve.

Serve with rice.

Beef and Lamb

Fresh Spinach With/Without Ground Meat

KIYMALI ISPANAK

2 pounds fresh spinach leaves and stems

3 tablespoons vegetable oil

1 tablespoon butter

1 large onion, chopped

1/2 pound ground meat, optional

1 large tomato, peeled and diced

1 teaspoon tomato paste

2 tablespoons uncooked short-grain white rice

Salt

Freshly ground pepper

SERVES 4 TO 5

This is a very simple but delicious dish cooked in almost every Turkish house in the winter when spinach is in season.

Pick over the spinach leaves, discard any damaged or blackened leaves. Cut 1/2 inch off the tips of the stems and discard any roots. Chop the spinach lengthwise into pieces 1 1/2 inches long. Place the spinach in a large bowl, cover with water, and let sit for 10 minutes. Pour the spinach into a colander (the sand will go to the bottom) and drain well. Rinse out the bowl, cover spinach with clean water, and repeat draining and changing water until there is no sand in the bowl (change water 2 or 3 times).

In a skillet heat the oil and butter, sauté onions, stirring, for 3 to 4 minutes. Add the meat, if using, and sauté another 3 to 4 minutes. Add the tomatoes, tomato paste, and rice and cook, stirring, for another 2 to 3 minutes. Add 1/2 cup of water. When it comes to a boil add the spinach and salt and pepper to taste. Cover and cook for 20 minutes on low.

Serve with yogurt and country bread.

Grape Leaves Stuffed With Meat and Rice

1 (16-ounce) jar grape leaves, drained

1 pound ground beef

1 teaspoon Red Bell Pepper Paste (page 37)

1 large onion, finely chopped

4 cloves garlic, finely chopped

$\frac{1}{2}$ cup uncooked medium-grain white rice

Salt

1 teaspoon black pepper

1 cup canned tomato juice

1 to 2 tablespoons vegetable oil

2 tablespoons tomato paste

2 tablespoons butter

MAKES 50 TO 60

SERVES 6 A MAIN COURSE

Place 5 cups of water in a saucepan and bring to a boil. Open any rolled grape leaves and place all leaves in the boiling water. Cook for 2 minutes and drain. Separate the leaves, remove the stems, and set aside.

In a large bowl mix together meat, bell pepper paste, onion, garlic, rice, 1 $\frac{1}{2}$ teaspoons salt, pepper, tomato paste, oil, and $\frac{1}{2}$ cup water (which makes the rice open up better). Mix well and set aside 10 minutes so flavors can blend with each other.

Take a grape leaf, rib side up, and put 1 teaspoon (or less according to the size of the leaf) rice filling along the bottom edge of the leaf. Fold the sides over the filling and roll up the leaf. Continue the same way with the remaining leaves. If some leaves are large, cut them vertically. Do not throw away any damaged or unused leaves, instead place extra leaves on the bottom of a large sauté pan. Then add the rolled grape leaves. If needed, place a second layer over the first, or even a third one if needed. Cover them with the remaining grape leaves and a piece of parchment paper. Put a plate upside down on top to weigh down the leaves.

Add tomato juice, 1 cup water, salt to taste, and dot with butter. Bring to a boil, reduce heat to simmer, cover, and cook 1 hour.

Remove from the heat and let rest 10 to 15 minutes. Serve with yogurt.

Nur's Note: These do not freeze well, but they will keep in the refrigerator for several days.

Beef and Lamb

Ground Meat With Fresh Peas

2 tablespoons butter

1 tablespoon vegetable oil

1 large onion, finely chopped

½ pound ground meat

2 tomatoes, peeled and diced

1 teaspoon tomato paste

2 pounds fresh peas, shelled

SERVES 4

Heat the butter and oil in a medium saucepan, add onions, sauté for 3 to 4 minutes. Add the ground meat and sauté for 6 minutes using the side of a wooden spoon to separate and cut up the meat as it cooks.

Add the tomatoes, tomato paste, mix well, and sauté 2 to 3 minutes. Add 2 cups of water and bring to a boil. Add the peas, reduce heat, and simmer covered for 50 minutes. If the peas absorb all the water and are still uncooked, add ½ cup of hot water and continue cooking.

Serve with rice and salad.

Ground Meat
on Skewers

1 pound ground beef or lamb

1 medium onion, grated

1/2 teaspoon salt

1/4 teaspoon ground pepper

2 teaspoons Aleppo pepper

2 tablespoons vegetable oil

SERVES 4

This is a variety of köfte.

Place the meat in a large bowl. Place a fine sieve or strainer over the meat and push and squeeze the onion against the sieve so the onion juice will fall on the meat. Discard the onion. Add the salt, pepper, Aleppo pepper, and oil to the meat and mix well with your hands. (The oil keeps the mixture soft since no bread is used.)

Divide the meat mixture into 8 balls. Place each ball on a skewer (flat ones are best) and shape into an oval. Gently squeeze the meat down the skewer, stretching it out until it is about 8 inches long and shaped like a hot dog. Rub gently between the palms of your hands to smooth the köfte. Lightly wet your fingers in water and using you thumb gently press along the length every inch or so making an indenture with your thumb and rotating the sides of the köfte. Repeat until all the köftes are done.

Heat the stovetop grill or barbecue grill. Place the skewers on the grill and cook for approximately 3 minutes per side.

Beef and Lamb

127

Island Meatballs

1 pound ground meat

3 slices stale bread, torn into
small pieces and crumbled

1 onion, grated

Salt

Freshly ground pepper

1 tablespoon dried oregano
or thyme

All-purpose flour

Vegetable oil

MAKES 16 TO 20

This recipe comes from the Turkish people who migrated from the Greek islands.

*I*n a large bowl combine the meat, bread, onion, salt and pepper to taste, and oregano. Lightly oil your palms, take a golf-ball size piece of the meat mixture, and roll gently between your palms until it is about 3 inches long.

Repeat until all the meat has been used. They should be about the length of a finger. Dip the köftes in flour, covering on all sides.

In a large skillet, heat the oil and fry the köftes for 3 minutes on each side. Drain well on paper towels and serve hot.

Köfte With Yogurt and Tomato Sauce on Pita Bread

YOĞURTLU KÖFTELİ KEBAB

3 slices stale (3 to 4 days old) white bread, with crusts removed

½ pound freshly ground lamb

½ pound freshly ground veal

1 medium onion, grated

2 cloves garlic, minced

1 teaspoon salt

½ teaspoon black pepper

½ teaspoon cumin

3 tablespoons finely chopped fresh parsley

¼ cup vegetable oil

4 long green chili peppers, kept whole and grilled with köftes

3 pita breads (½ piece for each person)

Tomato Sauce (page 40)

Yogurt Sauce (page 43)

TOPPING:
3 tablespoons butter, melted

1 teaspoon Aleppo pepper

MAKES 20 TO 24 PIECES

SERVES 6

Köftes taste much better with freshly bought ground meat.

Place the bread in a colander with a bowl underneath. Try to crumble the bread with your fingers and push it through the colander. If the bread is stale, it goes through very easily. Add the ground meats, onion, garlic, salt, pepper, cumin, parsley, and 3 tablespoons of the oil to the crumbled bread bowl. Mix well with your fingers, kneading it for at least 10 minutes.

Let mixture rest for 30 minutes then knead another 5 minutes. Wet your hands with the remaining 1 tablespoon oil, roll and shape into 3-inch long fingers.

Grill the whole chili peppers and the köftes or cook in a heavy nonstick frying pan until cooked through.

Preheat oven to 400°F.

Cut pita bread into 1-inch squares. Wrap them in a sheet of aluminum foil, seal tightly, put in the oven for 5 minutes. Remove from the oven and arrange them on 4 plates. Spoon tomato sauce equally over the pieces, then repeat using yogurt sauce. Divide the köftes equally on plates. Place a green pepper in the middle.

Beef and Lamb

129

Continued

In a small skillet melt the butter, add the Aleppo pepper, mix well, and drizzle over the plates and serve.

Nur's Note: Shish kebab is done exactly the same way as the köftes. You can have both shish kebabs and köftes together, if desired.

Ladies' Thighs Köfte

2 tablespoons uncooked
  medium-grain white rice

2 tablespoons extra-virgin
  olive oil

1 medium onion, finely
  chopped

1 pound ground lean beef

2 tablespoons chopped fresh
  Italian parsley

Salt

Freshly ground pepper

1/2 teaspoon ground allspice

3 tablespoons all-purpose
  flour

3 eggs, lightly beaten

1 1/2 cups sunflower oil for
  frying

SERVES 5

Pick over the rice for stones, rinse well, place rice in a pan with 1 1/2 cups water, and cook, boiling, until tender, about 10 to 12 minutes. Drain the rice and set aside.

In a skillet heat the olive oil and sauté the onions, add half of the meat, cook, stirring, until done. Drain off excess oil.

Place the onion and meat mixture in a large bowl. When mixture has cooled, add the remaining raw meat, the boiled rice, parsley, salt and pepper to taste, and allspice. Knead thoroughly, mixing well.

Take egg-sized pieces and wetting your palms with water, roll into balls, then flatten into ovals about 3 1/2 inches long by 1/2 inch thick. When all the köfte are ready, dip them into the flour and then into the beaten eggs.

In a large skillet, heat the sunflower oil over medium heat and fry the köftes until golden brown on both sides. Serve hot, or cold on picnics.

Beef and Lamb

Lamb Casserole With Chickpeas

ETLİ NOHUT

1 cup dried chickpeas

1 tablespoon butter

1 tablespoon vegetable oil

1 onion, finely chopped

½ pound lamb (leg) cut in
  ½-inch cubes

2 long hot green chili peppers,
  seeded, veined, and coarsely
  chopped

2 large tomatoes, coarsely
  chopped

1 teaspoon Red Bell Pepper
  Paste (page 37)

2 cups hot water

Salt

Freshly ground pepper

SERVES 4

Soak the chickpeas overnight in salted water to cover.

Drain the chickpeas, place in a pot, cover with water, and bring to a boil. Reduce heat to simmer and cook, uncovered, for 50 minutes. Drain well.

In a 3- to 4-quart pot, melt the butter and oil over high heat. Add the onions and sauté, stirring, for 5 minutes. Add the lamb and continue cooking and stirring on high heat for 3 to 4 minutes. Add the green peppers, tomatoes, and bell pepper paste. Stir to mix well, cook 2 more minutes, then add the hot water. Cover, bring to a boil, reduce heat to simmer, and cook for 30 minutes.

Add the drained chickpeas, salt and pepper to taste, cover and simmer for 40 to 45 minutes.

Lamb Ragout

2 tablespoons butter

1 tablespoon vegetable oil

1 pound lamb (leg), cut in
  1/2-inch cubes

20 pearl onions

3 cloves garlic, sliced in half

2 large tomatoes, peeled and
  coarsely chopped

Salt

Freshly ground pepper

1/4 teaspoon ground allspice

1/2 tablespoon white vinegar

SERVES 3 TO 4

*I*n a 3-quart pot heat the butter and oil. Add the lamb and cook on high heat for 5 minutes. Add the onions and garlic and sauté for 2 to 3 minutes. Add the tomatoes, and cook for 2 minutes. Add salt and pepper to taste, allspice, and vinegar, stirring to mix well.

Add 1 1/2 cups water, stir to mix well, bring to a boil, cover, reduce heat to simmer and cook for 60 minutes or until lamb is tender (another 10 to 15 minutes). If all the liquid has been absorbed, add a little more hot water before you continue cooking.

Serve with rice.

Lamb Shanks and Rice à la Ankara

6 lamb shanks (with bones)

I onion, peeled and kept whole

I bay leaf

6 to 7 black peppercorns

3 tablespoons butter

Salt

Freshly ground pepper

2 cups uncooked extra-long-grain white rice

TOPPING:

I tablespoon butter

2 tablespoons vegetable oil

4 tablespoons pine nuts

4 tablespoons currants

½ bunch fresh dill, finely chopped

SERVES 6

This is a rich meal with rice and meat. Served on special occasions, especially at weddings.

*I*n a large pot bring 8 cups of water to a boil. Add lamb, onion, bay leaf, and peppercorns. Boil 5 minutes, remove any scum, cover, and cook for I hour and 40 to 45 minutes on low-medium heat. Check the cooking liquid from time to time. If it is low add I or 2 cups of hot water as needed.

Preheat the oven to 350°F.

When meat is done place the shanks on a plate using a slotted spoon. Strain and measure the cooking liquid. Add enough water to the cooking liquid, if necessary, to make the 4 cups. Heat and add butter and salt and pepper to taste.

Arrange rice in a large ovenproof dish. Pour the hot liquid over the rice, and arrange cooked shanks on the rice (remove the large bones if desired, usually they fall apart after cooking). Cover tightly with aluminum foil and bake in the oven until the rice absorbs all the juice, about 20 minutes. Remove the dish from the oven and let it rest 10 to 15 minutes.

Meanwhile make the topping: heat the butter and oil in a saucepan, add pine nuts, and sauté, stirring, until they just begin to turn color, then add the currants and cook until nuts are golden brown. Remove pan from the heat, add finely chopped dill, spoon on the top of the rice and shanks, and serve. A green salad would be a good accompaniment.

Lamb With Eggplant

2 eggplants (2 pounds)

Salt

2 ½ tablespoons butter

I cup plus I tablespoon vegetable oil

2 pounds lamb (leg), cut in ½-inch cubes

2 onions, finely chopped

2 green bell peppers, seeded, ribbed, and cut in ¼-inch cubes

2 large tomatoes, peeled and coarsely chopped

Freshly ground pepper

2 tomatoes, cut in quarters lengthwise

I green bell pepper, seeded and cut lengthwise

SERVES 6 TO 8

Cut the eggplants in half lengthwise, then cut each piece lengthwise in 3 equal pieces. Cut each piece in thirds (this makes 18 pieces). Put the eggplant pieces in a colander, sprinkle with salt, let sit 30 minutes. Then wash well to remove the salt and pat dry with a paper towel.

In a 3-quart pot heat the butter the I tablespoon oil. When it starts sizzling, add the meat and sauté on high heat, cooking for 5 minutes or until the meat changes color. Add the onions, continue stirring for 3 to 4 more minutes, then add the bell pepper cubes and stir for I minute.

Add the tomatoes, salt and pepper to taste, and continue stirring for a couple of minutes more. Add 2 ½ cups water and mix well. Cover, bring to a boil, reduce the heat to a simmer, and cook for 60 minutes to 80 minutes more. Check to see if the meat is tender. Put meat in an ovenproof dish. Set aside.

Heat I cup oil and fry eggplant pieces until light brown. Remove them from the oil and drain on a paper towel.

Preheat oven to 400°F.

Arrange fried eggplant on top of the meat, leaving space in between slices for tomatoes and pepper slices. Alternate eggplant, tomatoes, and bell pepper slices, making a circular design. Bake for 20 minutes. Serve with rice and salad.

Beef and Lamb

Lamb With Spring Greens

7 tablespoons butter

2 onions, finely chopped

2 cloves garlic, finely chopped

6 lamb shank bones (4 to
  4 ½ pounds) with meat

I tablespoon all-purpose flour

6 cups warm water

Salt

Freshly ground pepper

I teaspoon sugar

2 carrots, cut in I-inch slices

5 spring onions, cut in I-inch
  strips

2 potatoes, peeled and cut
  into 8 pieces each

I head romaine lettuce, leaves
  separated and washed

I bunch Swiss chard, washed
  and stems removed

LEMON SAUCE:

2 egg yolks

Juice of I lemon

I tablespoon all-purpose flour

I cup plain yogurt

I tablespoon Drained Yogurt
  (page 42)

SERVES 6 AS A MAIN COURSE

This dish is prepared every spring when spring greens and spring lamb are available. It is one of the specialties of Turkish cuisine.

Melt butter in a large skillet and sauté onions and garlic for 5 minutes. Add the meat, and sauté for 5 minutes. Sprinkle the flour over everything and stir to mix well.

Add the warm water, salt and pepper to taste, and sugar. Cook, covered, over medium heat for I to I ½ hours. Check occasionally and if needed, add more water. Add the carrots and spring onions and cook, uncovered, for 10 minutes or until sauce boils. Uncover the skillet and reduce heat to medium. Add potatoes, lettuce, and Swiss chard leaves making sure the lettuce covers the meat and vegetables. Cook another 15 to 20 minutes.

Meanwhile prepare the lemon sauce. In a bowl whisk together I cup water, egg yolks, lemon juice, flour, and yogurts. Whisk to mix well. Whisk in ½ cup of the boiling liquid from the skillet, whisking constantly. When blended, add sauce to the skillet, whisk and cook for a couple of minutes. Remove skillet from the heat. Serve in soup bowls with the liquid from the skillet.

Lamb With White Navy Beans

KUZU ETLİ KURU FASULYE

1 cup white navy beans

1 tablespoon butter

1 tablespoon vegetable oil

1 large or 2 medium onions, finely chopped

2 long green hot chili peppers, seeded, veined, and coarsely chopped

2 large tomatoes, peeled and coarsely chopped

½ pound lamb (leg), cut in ½-inch thick cubes

3 cloves garlic, finely chopped

Salt

Freshly ground pepper

1 teaspoon Red Bell Pepper Paste (page 37)

3½ cups hot water

SERVES 4

A traditional dish of Anatolia.

Soak the beans overnight in salted water to cover.

In a 2- to 3-quart saucepan heat the butter and oil over high heat. Add the onions, and sauté for 5 minutes, stirring. Add the lamb and continue cooking for 3 to 5 minutes or until the meat changes color. Add the green peppers, tomatoes, garlic, and cook, stirring, for 2 minutes more. Add salt and pepper to taste, bell pepper paste, and 2 cups of hot water. Bring to a boil, reduce heat, cover, and simmer for 30 to 35 minutes.

Drain the soaking liquid from the beans. Place the beans in a pot with clean water to cover and bring to a boil. Reduce the heat and cook 30 minutes. Drain well.

Add the lamb mixture to the beans. Add 1½ cups hot water and mix well. Continue cooking on low heat for another 35 to 40 minutes or until lamb and beans are tender.

Lamb Wrapped in Eggplant Slices

2 to 3 large American
  eggplants

Salt

1 1/2 cup vegetable oil for frying

2 tablespoons stick butter

1 large onion, finely chopped

1-pound leg of lamb, cut in
  1-inch cubes

7 ounces canned tomatoes,
  diced, juice reserved

Freshly ground pepper

1 cup warm water

GARNISH:

2 tomatoes, sliced

1 green bell pepper, seeded,
  ribbed, and sliced lengthwise in 1/2-inch wide pieces

SERVES 6

Peel eggplant skins vertically in 1/2-inch strips from top to bottom at intervals for a striped effect (leaving one strip with peel and one without). Slice lengthwise in 1/4-inch-thick slices. Sprinkle every slice with salt and place in a colander. Set aside for 30 minutes (this removes the bitter juices). Wash eggplants and pat dry with paper towels.

Heat the oil and fry the eggplants until golden brown (in hot oil, it takes 2 minutes for each side). Remove the fried eggplants and place them on a tray covered with paper towels to drain well.

In a medium-size pan, melt the butter, sauté the onions, stirring, for 3 to 4 minutes. Add the lamb cubes, turn heat to high, add the tomatoes with juice, salt and pepper to taste, and 1 cup of warm water. Bring to a boil, reduce heat, cover, and simmer on low heat for 50 to 60 minutes or until the lamb is tender (it may take a little longer). When the lamb has cooked, cool, drain, set aside, and reserve the cooking liquid.

Preheat oven to 350°F.

In a 10-ounce glass bowl lay one slice of eggplant then place the other slice across the first (making a cross). Arrange each piece so the ends hang evenly over the sides of the bowl. Place 1/2 cup of cooked lamb in the center of the crossed eggplant slices. Fold the ends of one slice of eggplant over the lamb, then the end of the other piece so lamb is enclosed. Very gently turn the bowl upside down onto an ovenproof baking pan. Remove the bowl. Repeat with the remaining eggplants and filling.

Place a slice of tomato on each eggplant bundle, top with a slice of bell pepper, and spear them with a toothpick to hold them in place. Spoon all the leftover cooking juices (from the lamb) over the bundles and bake for 10 to 15 minutes.

Serve with rice.

Meatballs in Yogurt Sauce

¼ cup uncooked extra-long-grain white rice

¾ pound ground meat (half beef and half lamb)

3 eggs

½ teaspoon black ground pepper

¼ teaspoon ground cumin

1 tablespoon dried mint leaves

½ tablespoon salt

3 tablespoons butter, melted

Juice of 1 lemon

½ cup all-purpose flour plus 1 heaping tablespoon

1 cup plain yogurt

1 tablespoon paprika

SERVES 4

Wash the rice and let it sit in ¾ cup of water for 30 minutes. In a large bowl place the meat, 1 egg, pepper, cumin, ½ tablespoon dried mint, and salt. Mix well to blend. In a small bowl combine 1½ tablespoons of melted butter with ½ tablespoon mint.

In a small bowl, combine 1 egg and ½ of the lemon juice. In another small bowl mix together 1 heaping tablespoon flour, yogurt, 1 egg and remaining lemon juice.

Drain ½ cup of water from the rice and using your fingers crush the rice in the remaining water, breaking the rice up into smaller pieces. Drain the rice and add to the meat mixture, mixing well with your hands. Punch down the meat mixture a few times with your fist (this helps to mix and tenderize the meat).

In a large pot bring 5 cups of water to a boil. Pinch off small pieces of meat, ¾-inch to 1-inch and roll in between the palms of your hands to shape into a small ball. Repeat using remaining meat. You will make about 70 meatballs. Place ½ cup of flour in a large pan, add the meatballs, and shake them around the in flour quickly. Remove meatballs from the flour, and add all the meatballs at once to the boiling water. Cook over high heat, stirring occasionally. Cover the pot and cook until water returns to a boil.

Take ½ cup of the boiling water and stir it into the yogurt mixture, whisking constantly, then add another ¼ cup water, whisking (to mix well), and quickly whisk it into the soup. Whisk constantly for a minute and let the soup return to a boil. Cook, stirring occasionally, for 10 minutes. Place in 4 serving bowls.

Combine 1 ½ tablespoons of the melted butter with the paprika, mixing well. Combine the remaining 1 ½ tablespoons of the melted butter with 1 tablespoon of the mint, mixing well. Pour, swirling, a little paprika mixture in each bowl, and pour, swirling a little of the mint mixture.

Serve hot with rice.

Mom's Köfte From Tekirdağ

TEKİRDAĞ KÖFTESİ

3 slices stale (3 to 4 days old) white bread, with crusts removed

½ pound freshly ground lamb

½ pound freshly ground veal

1 medium onion, grated

2 cloves garlic, minced or finely chopped

Salt

Freshly ground pepper

½ teaspoon cumin

3 tablespoons finely chopped fresh parsley

¼ cup vegetable oil

MAKES 20 TO 24
SERVES 6

My mother Fahriye Dağli comes from Tekirdağ, a city in Thrace (part of Turkey on the European side). It is famous for its köftes. They are usually eaten with warm bread and yogurt. This is her recipe and our favorite childhood dish. Köftes taste much better with freshly brought ground meat.

Place the bread in a colander with a bowl underneath. Try to crumble the bread with your fingers and push it through the colander. If the bread is stale, it goes through very easily (or use a food processor). Add the ground meats, onion, garlic, salt and pepper to taste, cumin, parsley, and 3 tablespoons of the oil to the crumbled bread bowl. Mix well with your fingers, kneading it (by pressing down with your knuckles, turning it over) for at least 10 minutes. Let mixture rest for 30 minutes, then knead another 5 minutes.

Wet your hands with the remaining 1 tablespoon of oil and take a piece of meat the size of 2 walnuts, roll the meat into a ball, roll between your palms into a cylinder, shape into 3-inch-long oval patties. Press gently down to flatten somewhat. Grilled or cook the köftes for about 3 to 4 minutes per side, or until done, in a heavy nonstick heavy frying pan.

Nur's Note: Shape the köftes like walnuts and serve them as a warm snacks with drinks. I cook these party-size meatballs in a preheated 350°F oven for 20 minutes, shaking the tray from time to time. Cover them with foil as soon as you remove them from the oven to prevent color change. These can be made ahead and reheated. I serve them with mustard and ketchup.

Rack of Lamb

2 pounds rack of lamb (12 chops), French style

1 tablespoon chopped fresh oregano leaves, or 1 teaspoon dried

8 tablespoons vegetable oil

SERVES 4 TO 6

Cut the rack into individual chops, 1 bone per chop. Lay the chops on a piece of plastic wrap, cover with a sheet of plastic wrap, and pound the chops with a metal tenderizer to make them thinner.

Preheat the broiler.

Dip the chops in the oregano and pour oil over the chops, turning them over to coat the other side with oil. Cover the chops with plastic wrap and let them sit for 20 minutes at room temperature. Wrap a small piece of aluminum foil around the bottom of each bone. Broil 2 to 3 minutes each side or until done the way you like.

Shepherd's Sauté

3 tablespoons butter

3 tablespoons vegetable oil

I pound lamb (leg), cut into
  ½-inch pieces

I onion, cut into chunks

4 cloves garlic, cut in half

Salt

3 long green hot chili peppers, seeded and cut into
  ½-inch pieces

2 medium tomatoes, peeled
  and cut into chunks

I teaspoon fresh thyme

SERVES 4

This recipe is quick and easy.

*I*n a large skillet, heat I tablespoon of butter and all the oil over high heat. Add the meat and cook, shaking the pan instead of stirring, until the color of the meat changes. Add the onion and garlic and continue cooking and shaking the pan for another 2 minutes. Add salt to taste.

Add the remaining 2 tablespoons of butter, let it melt, add the green peppers and continue cooking by shaking the pan. Cook for I minute and add the tomatoes and thyme. Continue cooking and shaking the pan for another minute. Remove from heat and serve with a warm country bread.

Shish Kebab

1 large onion, grated

1 pound leg of lamb, cut 1
$^1/_2$-inch cubes

$^1/_2$ cup vegetable oil

2 onions, cut in 1$^1/_2$-inch by
1$^1/_2$-inch slices

1 or 2 long green hot chili
peppers, seeded

3 tomatoes, cut in quarters,
each quarter cut in half

SERVES 4

Squeeze the grated onion over the lamb.
Pour the vegetable oil over the meat and coat
meat on both sides, cover, and marinate
overnight in the refrigerator or for at least 6
hours.

Thread the lamb onto skewers, with 4 or 5
pieces of lamb per skewer. Next to each piece
of lamb, place 2 slices of onion, then a slice of
green pepper, then a slice of tomato. Repeat
until each skewer is threaded.

Heat the grill or broiler and cook the lamb for
about 10 minutes, turning to cook on all sides.

Beef and Lamb

Stuffed Cabbage Leaves With Chopped Meat

ETLİ LAHANA DOLMASI

3 small cabbages, 1½ pounds each

1 tablespoon plus 1½ teaspoons salt

1 pound ground beef

1 onion, finely chopped

4 cloves garlic, finely chopped

½ cup uncooked medium-grain white rice, washed and drained

⅓ cup finely chopped fresh dill

Freshly ground pepper

1 heaping teaspoon Red Bell Pepper Paste (page 37)

1 tablespoon tomato paste

1 to 2 tablespoons vegetable oil

1 cup chopped canned tomatoes with juice

MAKES ABOUT 50 PIECES

With a sharp knife cut out the cores of the cabbages.

In a large 6- to 8-quart pot, boil 4 quarts of water with 1 tablespoon salt and drop in 1 cabbage. Turn it periodically and push it down with a utensil. Cook the cabbage for 10 minutes, stirring and separating the leaves. Remove the leaves and place them in a large pot of cold water. Repeat, cooking the other cabbages, adding more boiling water as needed.

In a large bowl mix together the meat, onion, garlic, rice, dill, 1 teaspoon salt, pepper to taste, bell pepper paste, tomato paste, ½ cup water (this makes the rice open up better), and oil (this makes them shiny). Mix well.

Trim 1 inch from the bottom of each leaf. Carefully slice off as much as possible from the hard rib without cutting the leaf. If the leaves are really large cut them in half vertically. Place the leaves with the ribs facing down on the work surface and place a tablespoon of meat filling along the bottom edge of each leaf. Fold the sides over the filling and roll up the leaves. Place them on an ungreased jelly roll pan. Do not throw away any bad or torn leaves or extra leaves; instead place some on the bottom of a large sauté pan. Place the stuffed cabbage on them. If needed make two rows using the remaining extra leaves between the layers of the stuffed cabbage. Cover the stuffed cabbage with any remaining leaves.

Pour 1 1/2 cups water over the cabbages. Add the tomatoes with juice and 1/2 teaspoon of salt. Place a plate over the cabbage to weigh them down. Cover the pan and cook over high heat until liquid comes to a boil. Reduce heat and simmer, covered, for 40 minutes.

Stuffed Zucchini With Beef and Rice

10 large zucchini

½ pound ground beef

1 large onion, finely chopped

3 cloves garlic, finely chopped

¼ cup uncooked medium-grain white rice

2 tablespoons finely chopped fresh dill

1 tablespoon tomato paste

2 tablespoons vegetable oil

½ teaspoon salt

Freshly ground pepper

TOPPING:

2 medium tomatoes, peeled and coarsely chopped

1 tablespoon vegetable oil

1 tablespoon butter, softened to room temperature

Salt

Freshly ground pepper

SERVES 6

Vegetable (zucchini and eggplant) corers are available in Eastern or Mediterranean markets.

Peel the zucchini as thin as possible. It is best to use a scraper if you have one. Cut the zucchini in half and scoop out the inside with a long corer, leaving a ½-inch-thick shell.

In a large bowl combine the meat, onion, garlic, rice, ¼ cup water, dill, tomato paste, oil, salt and pepper to taste. Mix well and knead with your hands for 3 to 5 minutes. Let the mixture sit 10 minutes so the flavors can blend.

Stuff the hollowed out core of each zucchini with the meat mixture. Place the stuffed zucchini in a large sauté pan. Sprinkle the tomatoes over the zucchini, drizzle with the oil, and dot with the butter, salt and pepper to taste.

Pour 1½ cups of water around the zucchini cover with a parchment circle, press down on the circle, and cover the pan. Bring the water to a boil, reduce heat, and simmer zucchini for 20 to 25 minutes. Remove from the heat and let rest, covered, for 10 minutes.

Serve with yogurt.

Sultan's Favorite

2 tablespoons butter

1 tablespoon vegetable oil

1 large onion, finely chopped

1 1/2 pounds lamb (leg), cut in 1-inch cubes

1 green bell pepper, seeded, ribbed, and diced

2 large tomatoes, peeled and diced (or 1 cup canned, diced)

Salt

EGGPLANT PUREE:

2 pounds Asian eggplants

4 tablespoons butter

3 tablespoons all-purpose flour

1/4 teaspoon salt

1/2 cup milk

1 cup grated cheddar cheese

SERVES 4

This marvelous favorite of Topkapı Palace will become a favorite of yours too. It is not as time consuming as it looks and is certainly worth the time.

*I*n a 3-quart pot over high heat, heat the butter and oil. Add the onions and cook, stirring for 5 minutes. Add the lamb and continue cooking and stirring for 2 to 3 minutes. Add the bell peppers, tomatoes, and salt to taste, stirring to mix well. Add 1 1/2 cups water, mix well and continue cooking and stirring for 4 minutes.

Cover and bring to a boil. Cook for a minute or two, reduce heat to simmer, and cook, covered, for 1 hour and 10 minutes. Remove from heat.

While lamb is cooking prepare the eggplant puree. Pierce the eggplant all over with the tip of a small knife. Cook over a gas flame or grill, turning from side to side until the eggplant is tender and begins to ooze liquid. Remove the eggplants from the flame and gently tap all over the eggplants with the flat part of a knife blade. Hold the eggplants by the stems and carefully peel or slice away peel with a small sharp knife. Discard peels. Drain any excess liquid from the eggplants.

In a skillet melt the butter and whisk in the flour. Continue whisking for a minute or two. This makes a roux, a thickening agent for sauces. Add the salt, whisk to mix well, and add the eggplant flesh, mashing, whisking, and cooking until everything is well blended.

Beef and Lamb

Continued

Slowly pour in the half the milk, whisking the
whole time until well blended. Add the
remaining milk and continue to whisk and
cook until all the milk is absorbed and sauce is
thick. Remove the pan from the heat and stir
in the cheese, mixing well.

Pour the eggplant puree onto a large serving
platter, making a well in the center by pushing
the puree to the sides. Carefully spoon the
meat mixture and cooking liquid into the center of the puree and serve.

Sultan's Meatballs

PEYNİRLİ SULTAN KÖFTESİ

2 slices stale bread

1 pound ground veal or
  ground beef

1 tablespoon extra-virgin
  olive oil

1 egg yolk

1 teaspoon cumin

1 teaspoon dried mint

Salt

Freshly ground pepper

4 slices kasseri cheese or mild
  cheddar

SERVES 4

In the fifteenth and sixteenth centuries this was made for sultans in the Ottoman palaces.

Remove crusts and soak the bread in water for a couple of minutes. Squeeze dry and crumble. In a bowl place the ground meat, bread, oil, egg yolk, cumin, mint, and salt and pepper to taste. Mix well with your hands, kneading the mixture.

Divide the meat mixture into 8 hamburger-size pieces, and shape into patties. Place a slice of cheese on one hamburger, wet your hands and place another hamburger on the top of the cheese. Using your fingers, hide the cheese inside the 2 patties, pressing with your fingers to seal them together. Repeat with remaining patties and cheese. Oil the pan and grill them on both sides until done.

Beef and Lamb

Zucchini Moussaka

4 long zucchini

1/3 cup vegetable oil

1 onion, finely chopped

3 cloves garlic, finely chopped

1 green bell pepper, seeded, ribs removed, and chopped, optional

1 teaspoon salt

Freshly ground pepper

1/2 pound ground beef

8 stems and leaves fresh dill, separated and finely chopped

2 tomatoes, peeled and chopped

SERVES 6

This is a light summer dish. It can be made without the meat.

Nur's motto is: "do not waste anything!" Whenever fresh dill is used in a recipe, she also chops the stems and uses them in the dish for extra flavor.

Peel the zucchini, trim off the ends, and wash. Cut each zucchini in half and those pieces in half. Each piece will be about 2 inches long.

In a large skillet, heat the oil and sauté the onion, garlic, and bell pepper (if using) over medium heat. Cook, stirring, for 5 minutes and add the salt and pepper to taste. Stir and continue to cook, adding the meat. As you stir and mix use the side of a wooden spoon to chop the meat and separate the pieces. Cook until no pink shows in the meat. Add the dill (stems only) and tomatoes, stirring and cooking for another 3 minutes. Remove skillet from the heat.

In a 10- or 12-inch skillet, arrange half of the zucchini. Spoon half of the meat mixture over the zucchini, cover with the remaining zucchini, and then the rest of the meat.

Pour 1 cup of water over the meat, turn heat to high, and bring to a boil. When mixture has boiled for a minute, reduce heat to simmer, cover, and continue cooking for 20 minutes. When the zucchini is tender it is done.

Sprinkle the chopped dill leaves on top and serve.

Boereks and Breads

Auntie Melek's Spinach Boerek

SPINACH FILLING:

4 tablespoons vegetable oil

1 onion, finely chopped

1 pound frozen spinach leaves, thawed

Freshly ground pepper

1/2 pound white Turkish cheese or feta, crumbled

DOUGH:

1/2 cup butter, softened to room temperature

1/4 cup plain yogurt

1 1/2 tablespoons extra-virgin olive oil

1/2 teaspoon salt

2 cups plus 1 tablespoon all-purpose flour

FINISHING:

3/4 cup melted butter

1 egg yolk

2 tablespoons vegetable oil

2 to 4 tablespoons black sesame seeds

MAKES 42 PIECES

In a large skillet, heat the oil and sauté the onion for 5 to 7 minutes, stirring. Add the spinach and continue cooking another 7 to 8 minutes over medium heat. Add pepper to taste, mixing well. Remove the pan from the heat and let the mixture cool to room temperature. Crumble the cheese and add to the filling, mixing well. This can be done a day ahead.

Make the dough: in a large bowl combine the butter, yogurt, oil, salt, and 2 cups flour. Work ingredients together until they form dough (or use the food processor). If more flour is needed, add it a little at a time. Knead the dough for a few minutes on a lightly floured surface and divide the dough into 6 equal pieces. Roll each piece into a ball, cover, and let rest for 30 minutes.

Preheat the oven to 400°F.

On a lightly floured surface roll out each ball of dough, rolling in all directions, and turning the dough over a few times. Roll each circle until it is about 12 inches in diameter. Brush each circle with 2 tablespoons of melted butter.

Divide the filling into 6 portions, and place one portion down the center of the circle in a straight line (it will look like a log of spinach). Fold one half of the circle over the filling and roll up the boerek like a jelly roll or into a log.

Boereks and Breads

Place on a lightly greased cookie sheet. Repeat the process using remaining dough, butter, and filling.

Mix the egg yolk with the oil and brush the tops of it, Cut each log into 7 pieces, each about 1 ½-inches long. Sprinkle the tops with the sesame seeds and bake for 30 to 40 minutes or until golden brown.

Cigarette Boereks With Cheese

1 pound white Turkish cheese, crumbled

2 eggs, separated

1/2 bunch fresh parsley, washed, dried, and finely chopped

1/2 bunch fresh dill, washed, dried, and finely chopped

2 (1-pound) packages yufka (a type of Turkish phyllo) wedges

Vegetable oil for frying

MAKES ABOUT 84

Cigarette boereks are usually served as a side dish after a meat main course. They are also used as a snack with tea, or an appetizer at a buffet, cocktail party, or luncheon.

Soak the white cheese in cold water to remove the excess salt, drain, then mash with the egg yolks. Stir in the chopped parsley and dill mixing well.

Cut the wedge-shaped yufka sheets in half, lengthwise.

In a small bowl, lightly beat the egg whites. Rub a little egg white around the edges of the yufka except for the last 2-inches of the pointed end. Place a little filling at the base of each triangle and fold over the side edges of the bottom corners (triangle shaped pieces) to cover some of the filling. Fold the sides over like an envelope. Fold up the bottom edge to cover the filling and carefully roll up the yufka sheet like a cigarette (from the large end to the small point).

Wet the pointed end with a little water and press down to seal the boerek closed. Place the boereks on a cookie sheet and freeze until ready to cook. Remove from freezer and let sit at room temperature for 10 minutes.

In a large skillet place enough oil to measure 2 inches deep. Heat the oil and before frying the boereks, hold one between your fingers (vertically) and place it in 1/2 inch of the oil. If the oil is hot enough to cook with, bubbles will immediately form around the bottom of the boerek. Add as many boereks as the pan will hold in a single layer and fry the boereks turning once or twice, until golden brown all over. Place in a fine sieve to drain, then drain well on paper towels. Repeat until all the boereks are cooked and drained.

Boereks and Breads

Rose Boerek

2 tablespoons vegetable oil

1 large onion, finely chopped

1 pound frozen chopped spinach, thawed and well drained

1 package of 3 round sheets boerek pastry, at room temperature

3 tablespoons vegetable oil

1 teaspoon butter

6 tablespoons grated cheddar cheese

SERVES 6 AS A STARTER OR 3 AS A VEGETARIAN MAIN COURSE

A healthful favorite dish of working women, this is quick and easy.

*I*n a skillet, heat the oil and sauté the onion over high heat, stirring, for 5 minutes. Add the spinach and cook, stirring, for 3 to 5 minutes. Remove from heat and set aside.

Cut each large circular sheet of boerek pastry in half. Place ⅙ of the filling along the cut edge of each half circle and roll up like a jelly roll or log. Carefully begin to coil one end of the log, continuing until you have a "rose." Repeat, coiling the remaining pieces.

In a 9-inch Teflon skillet, heat 1 tablespoon (or more) of vegetable oil over high heat for a minute or two. Place 2 coiled roses in the pan (more if using a larger skillet) and turn heat to low. When roses are golden brown on the bottom, add the butter as you carefully turn them over, and continue cooking until the other side is golden brown. Repeat until all roses are cooked. Sprinkle each rose with a tablespoon of cheese and serve.

Seniha Ilkin's Puffing Boerek

SENİHA İLKİN'S PUF BÖREĞİ

1 egg

4 tablespoons extra-virgin olive oil

1 teaspoon cider vinegar

1 teaspoon salt

3 3/4 to 4 cups all-purpose flour (more if needed)

6 tablespoons butter, melted

Vegetable oil for frying

This recipe was taught to Nur by her mother-in-law, Seniha. These are addictive! Having a craving for some, Sheilah, being too lazy to make the dough from scratch, cheated and used thawed frozen puff pastry sheets. If you do not wish to fry the boereks you can bake puff pastry boereks in a 400°F oven for 15 to 20 minutes or until golden. However, the puffing ones use the dough below and should be fried.

In a large bowl combine 1 cup water, the egg, olive oil, vinegar, salt, and 3 3/4 cups flour. Work the ingredients together to make dough, or use a food processor. Knead the dough on a lightly floured surface for 5 minutes. Divide the dough into 2 pieces, roll each into a ball, cover, and let rest for 30 minutes.

Prepare the cheese filling by soaking the Turkish cheese in water for 20 minutes. Crumble and combine with the cheddar, parsley, dill and egg yolks, mixing well. On a lightly floured surface roll out one ball of dough, rolling in all directions (Nur uses a 24-inch piece of broom handle, 3/4 inch wide). Periodically roll the dough around the pin and roll it back and forth, then unroll it and continue rolling. Roll until you have a rectangular piece about 19 by 16-inches. Brush the entire top with 3 tablespoons melted butter. Fold one third of the left side over to the middle, and then fold from the right side to the middle. Fold this long piece in thirds, cover, and let rest for 30 minutes. Repeat with the other ball of dough.

Roll out the dough into a large rectangle 19 by 16-inches and place a tablespoon of the filling 1/2 inch up from the bottom edge. Place another tablespoon 2 inches from the first and continue along the edge. Carefully lift the edge of the dough up and over the tablespoons of filling, slightly stretching and rolling the dough as you go. Just use enough dough to cover the filling.

Boereks and Breads

159

CHEESE FILLING:

½ pound white Turkish cheese or feta

¼ cup grated cheddar cheese

½ bunch fresh parsley, finely chopped

½ bunch fresh dill leaves, finely chopped

1 or 2 egg yolks, lightly beaten

MAKES 50 PIECES

Using a round 3-inch cutter, or half of a drinking glass rim, cut half-moon shapes* with the filling in the center. Press to seal as you cut, or pinch and seal. Make sure they are well sealed. Cut away any excess dough and make a new row of filling. Repeat using all the dough and all the filling.

In a large skillet, heat enough vegetable oil to cover the bottom of the pan to a depth of ¼ inch. When the oil is hot enough, place some of the boereks into the oil. After a minute or two they will puff up. Fry, turning, until they are golden brown, then drain well on paper towels.

Repeat until all the boereks are fried. If you are not cooking the boereks immediately, place them on a parchment-lined jelly roll pan, cover tightly with plastic wrap, and freeze. Bring to room temperature and fry.

* You can use a small round ravioli cutter. Press, twist, and remove sealed boerek from the sheet of pastry.

Spinach Boerek

¼ cup vegetable oil plus 2 tablespoons vegetable oil

1 large onion, finely chopped

1 pound frozen chopped spinach, thawed and well drained

1 tablespoon butter

1 package of 3 round sheets boerek pastry

3 eggs

2 tablespoons Drained Yogurt (page 42)

½ cup milk

3 tablespoons butter, melted and cooled

Salt

1 teaspoon black sesame seeds

SERVES 6 TO 8

*I*n a skillet, heat 2 tablespoons of the oil and sauté the onion over high heat, stirring, for 5 minutes. Add the spinach and cook, stirring, for 3 to 5 minutes. Remove from heat and set aside.

Butter a 10-inch pie pan with the butter. Drape 1 large circle of pastry into the pie pan with excess hanging evenly over the sides. Shred the other 2 pastry sheets and divide into 2 piles.

In a bowl, whisk together the eggs, yogurt, ¼ cup vegetable oil, milk, 2 tablespoons melted butter, and salt.

Brush some of the egg mixture all over the pastry inside the pie pan and up the sides as far as the top of the pie pan. Place one pile of shredded pastry in the bottom of the pie pan (on top the sheet that is there) and wet with 4 or 5 tablespoons or more of the egg mixture.

Place the spinach mixture on top and spread evenly around the pan. Top the spinach with the other pile of shredded pastry, spreading it around, and wetting it with 4 tablespoons of the egg mixture.

Carefully tear off the excess large pieces hanging over the rims of the pie pan. Use them to cover the top of the boerek. Wet well with the egg mixture. Tear off any remaining pieces and lay them on top of the boerek and fold any edges

Boereks and Breads

over onto the top, covering with the remaining egg mixture. Set aside for 30 minutes so the liquid (egg mixture) can be absorbed.

Preheat oven to 400°F.

Sprinkle boerek with sesame seeds. Bake for 30 minutes or until golden brown on top.

Talash Boerek

(Meat Wrapped in Puff Pastry)

- 2 tablespoons butter
- I tablespoon vegetable oil
- I medium onion, finely chopped
- I pound stew beef, cut into ½-inch cubes
- 2 cubanel peppers, seeded and sliced crosswise
- I large tomato, peeled and diced
- 2 teaspoons tomato paste
- Salt
- Freshly ground pepper
- ½ teaspoon dried oregano
- 2 cups warm water
- I sheet frozen puff pastry, thawed
- I to 2 tablespoons milk

SERVES 4

This is an easy elegant dish (that can be used as a main course) for entertaining or for family. Nur also fills these with chicken or other favorite fillings instead of meat.

In a pot heat the butter and oil. Sauté the onions for 5 minutes, add the meat, mix well, and cook over medium heat for 3 minutes to sear in the juices of the meat. Add the peppers, tomato, tomato paste, salt and pepper to taste, oregano, and warm water. Bring to a boil, cover, reduce heat to medium and cook for an hour. You should have a thick sauce with meat and no juices. Depending on your stove, if you still have a lot of liquid left after 45 minutes, remove the lid, and cook, stirring, until all the liquid has been absorbed. Or you can drain any remaining liquid off and save it for a soup or sauce.

Preheat the oven to 350°F.

On a lightly floured surface roll out the puff pastry until it is approximately 15 inch square. Cut the pastry into 4 equal squares. Turn the squares so a point is facing you and squares now look like diamonds. Divide the meat filling among the pastry pieces. Bring the point nearest you up and over the meat. Bring the side points across the meat and the top point down, making an envelope over the meat. Turn the envelopes over and place on a cookie sheet.

Brush the tops of the envelopes with milk. Bake for 25 to 35 minutes or until golden brown. Serve at once.

Boereks and Breads

Turkish Manti

DOUGH:

2 cups all-purpose flour

1/4 teaspoon salt

1 egg, lightly beaten

FILLING:

1 small onion, grated

1 pound ground beef or veal

1/3 cup chopped fresh Italian
   parsley

Salt

Freshly ground pepper

YOGURT GARLIC SAUCE:

2 cups yogurt, at room
   temperature

2 to 3 teaspoons minced garlic

Salt, optional

PEPPER TOPPING:

2 tablespoons butter

1 teaspoon Aleppo pepper

Pinch of sumac, optional

SERVES 6 TO 8

Records show this dish has been served in Turkey since the late 1400s. It is the Turkish version of tortellini. This is a recipe we brought from Central Asia.

Prepare the dough by making a well in the flour, and adding the salt, egg, and 1/4 cup water in the center. Using your fingers, work the ingredients together until dough is formed. If needed, add more water a spoonful at a time. Knead the dough on a lightly floured surface until smooth and elastic. Gather into a ball, place in a bowl, cover, and let rest for an hour.

Prepare the filling by mixing together in a bowl the grated onion, meat, parsley, salt, and pepper to taste. Set aside.

In a small bowl combine the yogurt and garlic, with salt to taste if desired. Let sit at room temperature until ready to use.

Divide the dough into 2 balls. Roll out one ball of dough at a time on a lightly floured surface until very thin (about 1/16 inch). The secret of good dough is to roll it in different directions, not just in one direction. Cut strips 1 inch wide, then cut into 1-inch squares. (Nur cuts her manti into 1/2-inch pieces but filling them with pea-size pieces of filling and sealing them is very labor intensive, so I cut mine into 1-inch squares!) Place about a 1/2 teaspoon of filling in the center of each square. Bring the four corners together over the filling and pinch to seal. Continue making manti until all the dough and filling are used. Place the manti on a lightly floured surface to lightly coat them.

Bring a large pot of salted water to a boil and drop in half the manti. As soon as they are cooked they will rise to the surface. Remove them from the pot with a slotted spoon and place in a serving bowl or individual bowls with a tiny bit of the cooking liquid. Cover to keep warm while cooking the remaining manti.

Pour most of the yogurt sauce over the manti saving the rest to pass in a serving dish. Quickly heat the butter in a small skillet and when the butter is sizzling hot, quickly add the pepper, mixing well. Remove from the heat and drizzle over the yogurt sauce. Sprinkle with sumac if desired. Serve manti at once with yogurt sauce. Manti can be frozen.

Village Boerek

2 tablespoons vegetable oil

2 large onions, finely
chopped

I green pepper, seeded and
finely chopped

I pound ground beef

I tomato, seeded and finely
chopped

2 tablespoons chopped fresh
parsley

1/2 recipe Bazlama Bread
shaped into 12 balls
(page 170)

Butter, optional

MAKES 12

*I*n a large skillet heat the oil and sauté the onion and green pepper over medium heat, stirring, for 5 minutes. Add the meat and continue to cook, stirring and chopping with the side of the wooden spoon to separate the pieces of meat. Add the tomato and cook until no pink shows in the meat.

Drain the meat mixture to remove any excess liquid so the pastry will not get pasty. Stir in the parsley, season to taste, and let mixture cool.

Roll out the balls of dough, one at a time, on a lightly floured surface until 1/8 inch thick. Place filling on one half of the circle of dough and cover with the other half of the dough. Using your fingers crimp and pinch the edges together.

Heat a heavy 12-inch skillet over high heat and place one filled boerek in the pan. Heat until lightly browned on one side and turn and lightly brown on the other. Repeat using remaining filling and dough. These will not get puffy like the breads. Remove from pan.

If desired rub a little butter over the top (it will melt immediately) and serve.

Water Boerek

DOUGH:

3 ½ pounds all-purpose
  flour (12 ¼ cups)

1 tablespoon salt

12 eggs

¼ cup vegetable oil

1 cup cornstarch sifted with
  1 ½ cups all-purpose flour
  for rolling dough

½ cup vegetable oil

2 tablespoons salt

1 pound white Turkish
  cheese, crumbled

½ bunch fresh Italian parsley,
  finely chopped

½ bunch fresh dill weed,
  finely chopped

1 stick butter

2 cups milk

4 eggs

4 quarts ice water

MAKES 18 SQUARES

*This important delicacy is the Queen of boereks. According to
Ayla Algar in her* Classical Turkish Cooking, *"this
superb creation, jewel in the crown of the boerek family, is
the final and perfected outcome of the process that began
when Turks first rolled dough in their Central Asian home-
land almost a millennium ago." You will need a lot of time,
a large work area, a regular rolling pin, a ½- to 1-inch-
thick Turkish rolling pin, and two large pans (at least 16 by
12 inches).*

Make the dough: Place the flour in a large
bowl or on a work surface, make a well in the
center, and add the salt, eggs, 1 cup water, and
the vegetable oil. Mix well until a fairly stiff
dough is formed. Knead the dough on a lightly
floured surface for 10 minutes or until smooth
and elastic. Divide dough into 16 equal pieces
and shape each piece into a ball.

Line a large jelly roll pan with plastic wrap and
sprinkle a little of the cornstarch-flour mixture
on it. Cover tightly with plastic wrap and let sit
10 to 20 minutes until dough is springy.

In a large bowl mix together the cheese, parsley,
and dill and set aside.

In a large pot boil 4 quarts of water, the vegetable oil, and salt.

In a saucepan melt the butter, take a little and grease the bottom and sides of a
16 by 12 by 2-inch (or 13-inch) jelly roll pan. Place several bath towels next to
the jelly roll pan. Then add the milk to the pan of melted butter and cook for
a minute or two. Remove from the heat, and when it is warm enough to touch,

Boereks and Breads

16

whisk in the eggs, mixing well and set aside.

Sprinkle a work surface with a little of the corn-starch-flour mixture and roll each ball into a thin circle of pastry about 8 inches across, rotating the circle as you go to stretch the dough. Stack them in 2 stacks of 8, sprinkling the cornstarch-flour mixture over and in between each one. Using the rolling pin, flatten and stretch the stacks down, rolling until the stacks are 10 to 12-inches across. Starting at the end of the circle nearest you, wrap about 3 inches of the pastry around the Turkish rolling pin (or a 1 inch-thick dowel), sprinkling the cornstarch-flour mixture over it, and rolling this pin back and forth until the whole pastry is wrapped fairly tightly around the pin. When the first circle is wrapped around the pin, sprinkle with the corn-starch-flour mixture and start to add the second circle. Repeat until all 8 circles are wrapped around the pin one on top of the other. Roll each one off of the pin and restack the 8 circles. Repeat with the other 8 circles.

Roll each stack until the circles are about 18 inches across and very thin. Roll out each circle on some cornstarch-flour mixture, sprinkle the top of each circle with the mixture, and roll 8 of the circles around the pin again, sprinkling and unrolling. Circles should end up being about 20-inches across. Separate all the circles.

Preheat the oven to 400°F.

Drape 2 large circles in the jellyroll pan, allowing the edges of the circles to hang over the sides. Sprinkle the pastry with a little of the milk-butter mixture. Gently drop one of the circles into the boiling water for 3 seconds and quickly remove, using a large wire strainer or slotted spoon. Drop into the ice water, lift out, gently squeeze out any excess water, and place on the towels, opening the pastry up. Gently place the wet pastry sheet in the pan over the dry sheets. Using your fingertips, gently arrange the wet pastry in a crumpled (gathered) fashion. It is not suppose to lie flat. Remove any excess pieces. Sprinkle the wet sheet with a little of the milk-butter mixture. Continue cooking and layering until you have placed 5 wet sheets in the pan. As you work, add more boiling water to the pot as needed.

Spread the cheese filling evenly over the pastry. Cover with 2 uncooked layers of pastry. Continue cooking, layering, sprinkling with milk-butter mixture, 4 more of the remaining sheets. If the pastry appears to be taller than the pan, do not use so many sheets on top of the filling. Top with 2 dry sheets, removing any excess pastry. Bring the pastry that hung over the sides of the jelly roll pan up and fold over the top layer, stretching if necessary. Spread the top with some of the milk-butter mixture and bake for 30 minutes or until the top is golden brown. Carefully place another jelly roll pan of the same size over the boerek and carefully turn it over into the new pan. Continue baking for another 20 minutes until golden brown on top. Serve hot. If not using immediately, cool, cover, and refrigerate. Reheat before using.

Bazlama Bread

¼ cup dry yeast

3 ¾ cups warm water

1 tablespoon salt

7 to 8 cups all-purpose flour

MAKES 8 LARGE BREADS OR 24 SMALL

This is Necla Akgül's recipe. It can be halved.

*I*n a large bowl mix the yeast, ¾ cup warm water, and salt. Work ingredients together with your hand to blend. Add another cup of warm water and continue working. Add 7 cups of flour and an additional 2 cups of warm water and continue to blend everything together, kneading with your hands. If desired, knead the dough on a lightly floured surface. If additional flour is needed, add it. Shape dough into a large ball and wrap in plastic wrap.

Place wrapped dough back in the large bowl and place bowl on a blanket that has been folded in half vertically and place in a corner of your counter. Wrap the blanket all around the bowl and over the top of the bowl and let sit for 30 minutes or until the dough doubles in bulk. A large beach towel can also be used. This method will allow the dough to rise much faster.

Separate the dough into 8 balls, cover each one with plastic wrap, and let them rest on a lightly floured surface for 10 to 15 minutes. Roll each ball into a 9-inch circle, rolling in all directions until the circle is about ¼ inch thick.

Heat a heavy 12-inch skillet over high heat (no oil or butter is needed) and after it has heated for 5 minutes place one of the rolled circles into the pan. After a minute or two, turn the dough over. It will begin to blow up like a balloon. Turn another two times. Bread is done when puffed, very lightly browned, and with golden brown spots. Remove bread from the skillet and place on paper towels. Repeat using remaining balls of dough.

Firdevs' Black Sea Corn Bread

1 teaspoon vegetable oil

2 cups cornmeal

1/2 tablespoon salt

1 tablespoon butter, softened

2 cups boiling water

SERVES 4 TO 6

Simple and good.

Preheat the oven to 350°F for at least 15 minutes before baking. Grease an 8-inch round cake pan with the oil.

In a large bowl place the cornmeal, salt, and butter. Stir to mix well. Add the boiling water and continue to stir and mix until all the water is absorbed. Pour the cornmeal mixture into the prepared pan. Wet your hands and press the mixture down in the pan and smooth the top. With a sharp knife cut lines forming 1-inch squares.

Bake for 10 minutes then cover the pan with aluminum foil and bake for 15 more minutes. Carefully tip the bread onto a plate covered with foil, turning the bread over and place it back in the pan. Continue baking another 15 minutes or until golden and firm.

Boereks and Breads

Lahmacun

DOUGH:

2 ½ tablespoons dry yeast

5 ½ cups flour (more may be needed)

½ tablespoon salt

1 tablespoon sugar

½ cup vegetable oil

½ cup milk

*I*n a large bowl using your fingers, mix together the yeast and ¼ cup water. Mix well to dissolve the yeast. Add the flour, salt, sugar, ¾ cup water, and vegetable oil, mixing well.

In a small pan heat the milk just until it is warm but not hot. Add to the flour mixture and mix in, working the mixture until dough is formed. Knead as you mix. Gather dough into a ball, place in a bowl, cover with a kitchen towel, and let rise in a warm place for 60 to 65 minutes.

In a large bowl, combine all the filling ingredients. Cover and set aside. This can be made a day ahead, covered, and refrigerated. Bring to room temperature before using.

Divide the dough into 2-inch balls about the size of 2 walnuts. Place some oil on a work surface and oil your hands well. Take a ball of dough, dip it into the oil on both sides, and flatten it into a circle. Carefully using your middle 3 fingers, stretch the dough out in all directions until it is about 6 inches across. Place on a lightly oiled large cookie sheet or jelly roll pan and repeat with the other balls.

FILLING:

- 1 pound ground beef
- 1 bunch fresh Italian parsley, wash, dried, and finely chopped
- 3 large tomatoes, peeled and finely chopped
- 3 large onions, finely chopped
- 5 long cubanel peppers or 2 green bell peppers, finely chopped
- 2 to 4 cloves garlic, finely chopped or minced
- 1 teaspoon salt
- 1 teaspoon ground black pepper
- 3 tablespoons tomato paste
- 2 tablespoons Red Bell Pepper Paste (page 37)
- 4 tablespoons vegetable oil

MAKES 30 TO 36 PIECES

Preheat oven to 450°F.

Place about ¼ cup of filling in the middle of each circle and spread the filling out and to the edge of each circle. It is important that the filling go to the edge. Do not pile the filling on too thick.

Bake the pizzas for 10 to 15 minutes or until lightly brown on the bottoms and around the edges. Serve hot. Pizzas can be frozen after being cooled to room temperature.

Boereks and Breads

Stone Ground Whole Wheat Bread

TAŞTA ÖĞÜTÜLMÜŞ UNDAN SİYAH EKMEK

I tablespoon dry yeast dissolved in 2 tablespoons water

1⅓ cups water

¼ cup vegetable oil

I tablespoon honey

3½ cups stone ground whole wheat

¼ cup milk, at room temperature

I to 1½ teaspoons salt

MAKES I LOAF

This is Nur's favorite bread. She loves baking it and serving it to her friends.

*I*n a large bowl combine all the ingredients, mixing well until dough is formed. This can also be done in a mixer using a dough hook If dough is too sticky, a little more flour may be needed.

If you are going to knead the dough by hand, transfer the dough to a lightly greased work surface and knead by hand for 6 to 8 minutes. If using the mixer, continue to knead the dough for another 5 minutes with the dough hook.

Place the dough in a lightly greased bowl, cover with a towel, and let sit in a warm place until the dough doubles in size, about I hour. Then place the dough on a lightly floured surface and punch it down lightly. Place the dough in a lightly greased bread or loaf pan (approximately 9 by 5 inches), cover with a kitchen towel and let it rise again for another hour.

Preheat oven to 350°F.

Bake the bread for 40 minutes. If the top gets too dark before the baking is done, cover it with a piece of aluminum foil.

Pilafs

Ali Pasha Pilaf

1 ½ cup uncooked extra-
long-grain white rice

Salt

1 slice white bread, crusts
removed

½ pound ground beef

Freshly ground pepper

½ teaspoon Aleppo pepper

¼ cup vegetable oil

3 tablespoons butter

3 cups hot chicken broth

¼ cup pine nuts

SERVES 6

Soak the rice in 4 cups of warm water with a teaspoon of salt for 20 minutes, then drain.

Soak the bread in water, squeeze dry, and crumble. In a large bowl, mix the bread with the ground meat, salt and pepper to taste, and the Aleppo pepper. Mix well with your fingers, kneading the meat mixture. If necessary add ½ tablespoon vegetable oil (it will make it easier to shape the meatballs). Shape into tiny meat-balls, macadamia nut size.

In a saucepan heat the butter and sauté the rice. Add the hot chicken broth, salt and pepper to taste, bring to a boil, reduce heat and simmer for 15 to 20 minutes. Remove from the heat, place 2 layers of paper towels over the rice and cover. Let stand 10 minutes.

In a skillet, heat the remaining oil and sauté the pine nuts until golden brown. Remove with a slotted spoon and drain on paper towels. Add the meatballs to the oil in the pan, and sauté them by shaking the pan with the handle from side to side or around until all the meatballs are cooked. Remove the meatballs from the pan and drain on paper towels.

Brush the inside of a 4- to 5-cup ring mold with a little oil. Place the rice in the mold, press gently, and turn upside down on a round serving dish. Spoon the tiny meatballs into the center and decorate the rice with pine nuts. Serve with a salad.

Pilafs

Bulgur Pilaf

2 cups bulgur, (#4, not fine) unwashed

4 tablespoons butter

¼ cup vegetable oil

2 medium onions, finely chopped

2 small red bell peppers, seeded, ribbed, and finely chopped

2 large tomatoes, peeled, seeded, and chopped

1 tablespoon tomato paste

1 tablespoon Red Bell Pepper Paste (see page 37), optional

Salt

Freshly ground pepper

4 cups chicken broth or stock

SERVES 8

This can be eaten with Shepherd's Salad (page 75) and Ayran, or as an accompaniment to a main course (especially chicken dishes).

Pick over the bulgur and discard any impurities.

Heat the butter and oil in a saucepan and sauté the onions and bell peppers. Cook stirring for 5 minutes. Add the tomatoes, tomato paste, and bell pepper paste if using, stirring to mix well, and cook another 5 to 6 minutes. Add salt and pepper to taste, and mix well. Add the chicken broth and bring to a boil. Add the bulgur, stir, cover, and return to a boil. Reduce heat to low and simmer, covered, until the liquid has evaporated and steam holes appear in the surface of the bulgur.

Remove the pot from the heat, remove the lid, and cover the pot with a dry dish towel or paper towels. Replace the lid and let stand for 10 to 15 minutes. Stir with a wooden spoon from the sides inward so that the grain separates. Cover the pot and let it stand for another 5 minutes, and place on a serving dish and serve.

Eggplant With Rice

Salt

1 pound eggplant or 3 to 4
  Italian eggplants

1 cup vegetable oil for frying

1/3 cup extra-virgin olive oil

2 onions, finely chopped

1 cubanel pepper, cut in
  1 by 1/8-inch strips or
  1/2 green bell pepper
  seeded and cut into strips

1 medium tomato, peeled
  and finely chopped

1 cup extra-long-grain white
  rice

1 teaspoon sugar

1 teaspoon ground allspice

1/4 teaspoon ground cinnamon

2 tablespoons fresh finely
  chopped dill weed

SERVES 4

Soak the rice in salted warm water for 30 minutes.

Remove the stems of the eggplant. Peel eggplant skins vertically in 1/2-inch strips from top to bottom at intervals for a striped effect (leaving one strip with peel and one without) and slice them into 1-inch square pieces. Sprinkle slices with salt and place in a colander. Let sit 30 minutes then wash eggplants and pat dry with paper towels. Set aside about 15 pieces for decorating the finished dish.

Heat the vegetable oil in a large skillet and fry the eggplant pieces for 2 to 3 minutes on each side. Drain well on paper towels and set aside.

Heat the olive oil in a large sauté pan and cook the onions over medium heat for 10 minutes. Add the bell pepper and tomato and cook 2 to 3 minutes, mixing well. Drain the rice and add it, cooking over low heat for 3 to 4 minutes. Add 1 teaspoon salt, sugar, allspice, cinnamon, and 2 cups of water. Mix well, cover, and cook for 10 minutes. Add the eggplant pieces, cook 1 minute, mixing well, and remove pan from the heat. Place a paper towel between the pan and the lid. Replace the lid, and let sit for 30 minutes. Mix well, replace the lid, and let sit another 30 minutes.

Place the reserved eggplant pieces in the bottom of a 5-cup Pyrex bowl. Place the cooked rice mixture on top and press gently down to pack the mixture. Let it sit for 5 minutes. Place a serving plate on top of the bowl and turn it upside down onto the plate. Remove the bowl. Sprinkle with dill weed and serve at room temperature.

Pilafs

179

Green Lentil and Bulgur Pilaf

MERCİMEKLİ PİLAV

2 cups green lentils

²/₃ cup extra-virgin olive oil

3 medium onions, finely chopped

Salt

Freshly ground pepper

1 tablespoon Red Bell Pepper Paste (page 37; if not available, increase tomato paste to 3 tablespoons)

2 tablespoons tomato paste

1 cup bulgur (do not wash)

1 chicken bouillon cube

SERVES 10 TO 12
AS A SIDE DISH

For a vegetarian this is a nice main course accompanied by a salad, and if desired, the recipe can be cut in half. There is a custom called Dardar Baba Table connected with this recipe among some Turkish people. When you make this dish you can invite friends to participate in a small ceremony. You light a candle for each wish you want to make and say a small prayer and let the candle burn for a minute or two. Then you blow it out and carefully wrap it in a paper towel or napkin with the name of the person or thing you wished for written on it. Then you eat the lentils and drink some Ayran. When one of your wishes comes true, you light the specific wish candle again and cook green lentils and drink Ayran with your friends to give them the opportunity to make a wish and light a candle. If a wish has not come true you do not relight its candle.

Soak the lentils in hot water for 2 to 3 hours then drain well.

Cook the lentils in a pot with 5 cups of water until tender. Drain well and set aside.

In a 5- or 6-quart pot heat the oil over medium heat and sauté the onions, stirring, for 10 minutes. Add salt and pepper to taste, bell pepper paste if using, tomato paste, 2 cups water, lentils, bulgur, and chicken bouillon cube. Stir, mixing well, and reduce heat to simmer. Cover the pot and continue cooking over low heat, stirring occasionally, for 20 minutes. Turn off the heat and place paper towel between the pot and the lid to absorb all the steam. Let pilaf rest for a few minutes then serve. This can be eaten hot, warm, or cold.

Lamb With Rice, Carrots, and Nuts

KUZU ETLİ HAVUÇLU PİLAV

LAMB:

1 tablespoon vegetable oil

1 ½ pound leg of lamb, cut in 1-inch cubes

1 onion, peeled and kept whole

Salt

Freshly ground pepper

4 cups hot water

RICE:

2 cups uncooked extra-long-grain white rice

4 tablespoons butter

1 onion, finely chopped

1 pound carrots, julienned (or coarsely grated)

2 teaspoons tomato paste

Freshly ground black pepper

½ teaspoon ground cinnamon

½ teaspoon ground allspice

Ingredients continue on page 182

This rice was brought to the southeast part of Turkey by the Uzbeks and the Turkmens who migrated and settled there. The use of almonds and pistachios was added later. This is excellent for a main course, and for buffet meals. You can also cook this rice without the lamb and serve it as a side dish with any main course.

Heat the oil in a large skillet over medium heat. Add the lamb cubes, cook, stirring for 6 to 7 minutes or until all lamb cubes change color. Add the onion, salt and pepper to taste, and the hot water. Let mixture boil for a minute, reduce heat, and simmer on medium-low heat for 45 to 60 minutes. For the best results, take one piece of meat and try it. If it is not tender enough you can continue cooking for an extra 5 or 10 minutes.

Soak the rice in warm water for 15 to 20 minutes.

In a saucepan, melt the butter and stir in the onion. Stir and sauté for 3 to 4 minutes then add the carrots. Continue cooking another 6 to 7 minutes, until a yellowish color (from the carrot) comes out. Add the rice, mix well, and cook another 3 to 4 minutes.

Measure the broth from the lamb. If there is not 4 cups, add enough warm water to equal 4 cups. Add to the rice. The moment it starts boiling, add the cooked lamb (remove the whole cooked onion), tomato paste, and taste before adding salt and paper. Be careful as there is salt and pepper in the broth.

Continued

TOPPING:

1 cup vegetable oil

½ cup whole blanched
  almonds*

½ cup blanched pistachios*

**SERVES 8, FOR BUFFET MEALS
SERVES 10 TO 12**

Cover and simmer the rice on low heat until all liquid is absorbed and steam holes appear on the surface, 15 to 20 minutes. Turn off the heat and sprinkle rice with cinnamon and all-spice. Cover with a dry kitchen towel or 2 paper towels and replace the lid. Let mixture stand 15 minutes, then stir with a wooden spoon from the sides inwards so that the grains separate and spices blend well. Place the rice in a serving dish.

While rice is cooking, make the topping: place the cup of oil in a shallow frying pan, heat well, add the almonds first, and fry them for 3 to 5 minutes. They should be a golden/pink color. Remove them from the oil, and drain on paper towels. Then add the pistachios, fry them for 2 to 3 minutes, (since the oil is still hot, they need less frying). Remove nuts from the oil and drain well on paper towels. You can do this ahead of time and keep them in an airtight jar. Decorate the top of the rice with fried almonds and pistachios.

* If you can't find blanched nuts, cook nuts with their skins in boiling water for 5 minutes, drain, and place on a kitchen towel. Rub part of the towel back and forth over the nuts to remove the skins.

Rice With Carrots and Saffron

KIYMALI HAVUÇLU PİLAV

½ cups uncooked extra-
long-grain white rice

1 teaspoon salt

4 tablespoons butter

2 tablespoons vegetable oil

2 medium onions, finely
chopped

½ pound ground beef

½ pound carrots, julienned

3 cups chicken broth

Salt

Freshly ground pepper

⅓ teaspoon saffron

SERVES 6

This dish is a specialty of Eastern Turkey.

Soak the rice in 4 cups of warm water, with 1 teaspoon of salt, for 20 minutes, then drain.

In a heavy saucepan heat butter and oil, add onions and ground beef. Sauté for 10 minutes. Add the carrots and continue cooking, stirring for another 5 to 6 minutes. Add chicken broth, bring to a boil, add rice, salt and pepper to taste, and saffron. Simmer, covered, 15 to 20 minutes or until all the broth is absorbed. Turn off the heat, uncover, put 2 layers of paper towels over the mixture and cover. Let rest 10 minutes, mix with a wooden spoon and serve.

Rice With Chickpeas

1 ½ cups uncooked extra-long-grain rice

Salt

4 tablespoons butter

1 tablespoon vegetable oil

1 (15.5-ounce) can chickpeas, washed and drained

Freshly ground pepper

3 cups hot chicken broth

SERVES 6

Soak rice in 4 cups of warm water with 1 teaspoon of salt for 20 minutes, then drain.

In a saucepan heat butter and oil, and sauté chickpeas for a minute. Add salt and pepper to taste and chicken stock. Bring to a boil, add rice, cover, and simmer 15 to 20 minutes until all broth is absorbed. Turn off the heat and arrange 2 layers of paper towels over the surface of the food. Cover again, and let rest for 10 minutes. Mix gently with a wooden spoon and serve.

Rice With Currants and Pine Nuts

1½ cups uncooked extra-long-grain white rice

Salt

½ bunch dill stems and leaves, washed

½ bunch stems parsley and leaves, washed

4 tablespoons butter

2 tablespoons vegetable oil

1 large onion, finely chopped

5 tablespoons pine nuts

4 tablespoons currants

2 tablespoons dry mint

½ teaspoon ground allspice

Freshly ground pepper

3 cups hot chicken broth

SERVES 6

A rice dish for special occasions.

Soak rice in 4 cups of warm water with 1 teaspoon of salt for 20 minutes, then drain. Separate the dill stems and leaves. Finely chop each separately and set aside. Separate the parsley stems and leaves. Finely chop each separately and set aside.

In a saucepan heat butter and oil, add onions and sauté for 5 minutes, add pine nuts and continue sautéing another 5 to 6 minutes. Add rice and continue cooking another 2 to 3 minutes, mixing well.

Add currants, mint, allspice, salt and pepper to taste, and stems of dill and parsley. Mix well and add chicken broth, bring to a boil, reduce heat and simmer, covered, for 15 to 20 minutes or until all water is absorbed. Turn off the heat, uncover, place 2 layers of paper towel over the rice, cover, and let stand 10 minutes.

Mix in dill and parsley leaves and serve.

Rice With Peas

1 cup uncooked extra-long-
   grain white rice

Salt

3 tablespoons butter

1 tablespoon vegetable oil

$\frac{1}{2}$ cup frozen peas

Freshly ground pepper

2 cups chicken broth

SERVES 4

Soak rice in 3 cups of warm water with 1 tea-spoon of salt for 20 minutes, then drain.

In a saucepan heat the butter and oil, add the peas and sauté for 2 to 3 minutes. Add salt and pepper to taste and chicken broth, mixing well. Bring to a boil, add rice, and simmer, cov-ered, for 15 to 20 minutes or until all the broth is absorbed. Turn off the heat, uncover, place 2 layers of paper towels over the rice, and cover again. Let stand 10 minutes. Mix with a wooden spoon and serve.

Rice With Vermicelli and Almonds

ŞEHRİYELİ BADEMLİ PİLAV

1 cup uncooked extra-long-grain white rice

Salt

¾ cup vegetable oil for frying almonds

½ cup whole blanched almonds

3 tablespoons butter

¼ cup broken vermicelli

2 cups chicken broth

Freshly ground pepper

SERVES 4 TO 6

Among my guests, this has become one of the most popular dishes. Actually, it is a very simple way of cooking rice. Adding almonds is my contribution and makes the rice taste better and look richer.

Soak rice in 3 cups of warm water with 1 teaspoon of salt for 20 minutes, then drain.

Heat the oil in a medium-size frying pan. Fry the almonds carefully, stirring until they are golden brown. Be very careful as they can brown quickly. Remove from the oil and let cool and drain on paper towels. Reserve the oil.

In a medium saucepan heat butter and 2 tablespoons of reserved oil. Sauté the vermicelli, stirring, until golden brown. Add chicken stock, salt and pepper to taste, and bring to a boil. Add the rice, reduce heat to simmer, and cook, covered, for 15 to 20 minutes or until all broth is absorbed. Remove from the heat. Place two layers of paper towels on the rice, cover, and let stand 10 to 15 minutes. Uncover and mix well.

Place the almonds on the bottom of a 4- to 5-cup Pyrex bowl. Place rice on the almonds and lightly flatten with a wooden spoon. Let it rest a couple of minutes then turn upside down on a serving dish.

Tomato Rice Pilaf

1 cup uncooked extra-long-grain white rice

1 teaspoon salt

2 tablespoons butter

2 tablespoons vegetable oil

2 medium tomatoes, peeled and finely chopped

Salt

Freshly ground pepper

2 cups hot chicken broth

SERVES 4

Soak the rice in a bowl with the salt and 3 cups of warm water for 20 to 30 minutes, then drain well.

In a saucepan heat the butter and oil, add the tomatoes, and sauté for 4 to 5 minutes. Stir in the rice, mix well, add the salt and pepper to taste, and the chicken broth. Mix well, bring to a boil, reduce heat to simmer, cover, and cook 15 to 20 minutes or until the rice absorbs all the broth. Remove from the heat, place 2 layers of paper towels on the rice, cover the pot, and let stand for 10 minutes in a warm place. Mix well with a wooden spoon and serve.

Uzbek Pilaf

2 cups uncooked extra-long-grain white rice

1 tablespoon salt

1 pound leg of lamb, cut into 1-inch cubes

2 tablespoons butter

2 medium onions, finely chopped

3 medium carrots, coarsely grated

1 teaspoon salt

Freshly ground pepper

½ teaspoon ground allspice

½ teaspoon ground cinnamon

SERVES 6 TO 8

The name comes from the Uzbek people of Central Asia.

Pick over the rice and place in a bowl. Cover with hot water and stir in salt. Let rice stand for 30 minutes, then rinse thoroughly until the water runs clear.

In a large pot, bring 6 cups of water and the lamb to a boil, reduce heat, simmer, skimming occasionally, and cook until the meat is tender, about 60 minutes. Strain the liquid off and reserve for later use.

In a skillet, melt the butter and gently fry the onions. Add the cooked meat, stir to mix well, and cook for a few minutes. Add the carrots and stir briefly with a wooden spoon. Add 2 ½ cups of the warm meat stock and salt and pepper to taste. Bring to a boil, add the rice, stir, and lower the heat to simmer. Cover and cook until steam holes appear in the surface of the rice, about 15 to 20 minutes. Remove from the heat, cover with a dry kitchen towel and replace the lid. Set aside for 10 to 15 minutes. Stir in the allspice and cinnamon and serve hot.

Pilafs

189

Veiled Rice

1 ½ cups uncooked extra-long-grain rice

Salt

1 small chicken or 4 chicken legs (1 ½ to 2 pounds)

1 onion, peeled and kept whole

1 small carrot, peeled and kept whole

6 black peppercorns

1 bay leaf

Freshly ground pepper

¼ cup vegetable oil

3 tablespoons pine nuts

⅔ cup whole blanched almonds

3 tablespoons butter

1 sheet frozen puff pastry, thawed

1 to 2 tablespoons milk

SERVES 6 AS A MAIN DISH, 8 AS A SIDE DISH

This is a specialty of Siirt in South Eastern Turkey. It can be used as a main dish as well as a side dish.

Soak the rice in a bowl with 4 cups of warm water mixed with 1 teaspoon of salt. Let sit 20 minutes, then drain well.

Wash and drain the chicken, removing any excess fat. Place 5 cups of water in a large pot, add the onion, carrot, peppercorns, bay leaf, salt and pepper to taste. Bring to a boil, add the chicken, cover, reduce heat to medium-low, and cook about 40 minutes or until chicken is done. Remove the chicken from the pot, cool, remove skin and bones, and shred into 2 ½- to 3-inch pieces. Set aside. Strain the broth and save for the rice.

In a small skillet, heat the oil and carefully fry the pine nuts until golden brown. Remove them quickly from the pan with a slotted spoon and drain well on paper towels. Fry the almonds in the same oil until golden brown, remove from the oil, and drain well. Set nuts aside.

In a large saucepan heat the butter and sauté the rice. Add salt and pepper to taste, 3 cups reserved chicken broth, and bring to a boil. Reduce heat, cover, and cook 13 minutes. Add the chicken pieces and the nuts. Mix well with a wooden spoon. Remove the pan from the heat. Cover the mixture with 2 layers of paper towels, replace the lid, and let mixture cool for 15 to 20 minutes.

Preheat oven to 350°F. Grease a 5- or 6-cup
Pyrex bowl. On a lightly floured surface roll
out the pastry until it is approximately 15-
inches square. Drape the pastry into the Pyrex
bowl with the excess hanging evenly over the
edges. Fill the pastry with the rice and chicken
filling, pressing down gently to pack it. Fold
the draped pastry over the filling, removing
any excess pastry. Press down gently on the
sealed pastry and brush the top with a little
milk.

Bake veiled rice for 40 minutes or until gold-
en brown. Place a 9- or 10-inch pie plate over
the top of the Pyrex bowl and turn the veiled
rice over onto the pie plate so the dome is now
on top. If not lightly golden brown, return to
the oven and continue baking until it is
(another 5 to 10 minutes).

White Rice

1 cup uncooked extra-long-grain white rice

Salt

2 cups chicken broth

3 tablespoons butter

1 tablespoon vegetable oil

Freshly ground white pepper

SERVES 4

Soak rice in a bowl with 1 teaspoon of salt and 3 cups of warm water for 20 to 30 minutes, then drain.

In a saucepan bring chicken broth, butter, oil, salt and pepper to taste, and rice to a boil. Boil for 2 to 3 minutes, cover, and simmer on low heat 15 to 20 minutes, or until rice absorbs all the water. Turn off the heat and uncover the pan. Place 2 layers of paper towels over the rice, cover, and let stand 10 minutes. Uncover, mix well, and spoon the rice into a serving dish.

Nur's Note: Long-grain and extra-long-grain white rice absorb more liquid than medium-grain white rice.

Vegetables

Artichoke Hearts With Vegetables

4 large fresh artichokes

1 1/2 lemons

1 tablespoon all-purpose flour

1/4 cup of extra-virgin olive oil

1 large onion, finely chopped

2 small carrots, diced into 1/4-inch squares

1 medium potato, peeled and diced into 1/4-inch squares

1/3 cup frozen peas

Juice of 1/2 lemon

1 teaspoon salt

2 teaspoons sugar

2 tablespoons finely chopped fresh dill weed

SERVES 4

This is a spring vegetable, a very light and delicious starter. Ideal for special occasions.

Remove all the outer leaves of the artichokes leaving only the tender ones. Trim off the tops of the remaining leaves, leaving about 2 inches attached to the heart. Trim the stalks, and slice. Then with a small knife horizontally slice away the purple choke and pare away any inner leaves and hard sections until the white heart is left. Finally, remove any fine hairs from the choke with a spoon.

In a bowl put 2 cups of water, juice of 1 lemon, and flour, mixing well. Add the peeled artichokes and let sit (this prevents discoloring) for 15 to 20 minutes.

In a large sauté pan or skillet heat the olive oil and sauté the onions for 5 minutes, stirring, then add the carrots and continue cooking for 5 more minutes. Add potatoes and peas and sauté for a minute. Drain the artichokes and add them to the vegetables along with 2 cups of warm water, juice of 1/2 lemon, salt, and sugar. Place a wet parchment circle over the entire surface of the saucepan, cover, and cook over low-medium heat about 35 minutes or until tender (you can check artichokes with a toothpick).

Remove pan from heat and let everything cool in the pan. Place the artichoke hearts in a serving dish and fill them with a tablespoon of vegetables, placing remaining vegetables to the sides, and sprinkle with chopped dill.

Vegetables

Cabbage

1/4 cup vegetable oil

2 tablespoons butter

1 onion, finely chopped

2 cloves garlic, finely chopped

2-pound cabbage, shredded

1 green bell pepper, seeded, ribbed, and chopped

1 red bell pepper, seeded, ribbed, and chopped

1/2 tablespoon Red Bell Pepper Paste (page 37)

Salt

Freshly ground pepper

1/2 cup coarse bulgur

1/2 tablespoon tomato paste

1 tablespoon chopped fresh parsley

Yogurt, optional

SERVES 4 AS A MAIN DISH, 6 TO 8 AS A SIDE DISH

A vegetarian side dish or main course, this dish can also be made with meat.*

*I*n a large skillet, heat the oil and butter. Sauté the onions and garlic over high heat, stirring, for 3 to 5 minutes. Do not let them brown. Add the cabbage and bell peppers and stir to mix well. Keep turning pieces and stirring.

Add the bell pepper paste and salt and pepper to taste. Mix well and continue cooking and stirring. Add the bulgur, tomato paste, parsley, and 1/4 cup water. Stir and cook 2 minutes. Cover, turn heat to low, and cook for 10 minutes then remove from the heat. Serve hot or warm. Good served with yogurt.

*If you want to use meat, omit the bulgur and add 1/2 pound ground meat after you sauté the onions and garlic. Sauté the ground meat for 5 minutes, then add the cabbage and peppers.

Celery Root With Vegetables

ZEYTİNYAĞLI KEREVİZ

⅓ bunch fresh dill

1½ pounds celery root, peeled

⅓ cup extra-virgin olive oil

21 small pearl onions

3 carrots, cut in ½-inch cubes

1 medium potato, peeled, diced, and cut in ½-inch cubes

½ cup frozen peas

½ teaspoon sugar

Salt

SERVES 8

Since celery contains high fiber, this is a very healthy dish.

$\mathcal{F}$inely chop the stems of the dill weed and set aside. Finely chop the dill weed and set aside.

Slice off the 4 rounded sides of the celery root so it looks like a large cube. Slice the root in ½-inch slices. With a small knife round off the edges so the slices become round. Be careful not to cut through the bottom. Scoop out a 2-inch circle from the center of each slice (like a shallow bowl).

Heat the oil in a large saucepan over medium-heat and sauté the onions for 4 to 5 minutes. Add the celery slices, dill weed stems, carrots, and continue cooking for another 2 minutes. Add 2 cups of water, cover, and cook for 10 minutes on medium-heat. Then add potatoes, peas, salt, and sugar. Mix well.

Cut a parchment paper circle to fit over the vegetable mixture (this prevents color change). Place it on top the vegetables, press it down. Cover the pan and simmer for 30 to 45 minutes or until celery root is tender and a toothpick goes through it easily. Celery root should be soft. If not, continue cooking.

Remove the pan from the heat and let it rest, covered, for 2 hours (so the celery root does not fall apart) until celery roots are cool to the touch. Place the slices of celery root on a serving platter and spoon the vegetables and liquid onto each slice. Sprinkle with chopped dill and serve.

Vegetables

Cranberry Beans Pilaki

1 cup dry cranberry beans

2 teaspoons salt

1/4 cup of extra-virgin olive oil

1 medium onion, finely chopped

2 cloves garlic, coarsely chopped

1 green bell pepper, seeded, ribbed, cut in strips

2 small carrots, sliced round crosswise

1 stalk celery, thinly sliced

2 medium tomatoes, peeled and chopped

1 medium potato, peeled and diced in squares

1 teaspoon sugar

GARNISH:

2 tablespoon chopped parsley leaves

1 lemon, cut in quarters lengthwise

SERVES 4 TO 6 PEOPLE AS A STARTER

Cranberry beans are sometimes called borlotti or Roman beans. They have a slightly nutty taste. Originally they are from South America and from there made their way to Europe. Cannellini, pinto, or red or pink kidney beans can be used as substitutes.

Soak the beans in salt water overnight.

Drain the beans, boil them in 3 cups of water with 1/2 teaspoon of the salt for 10 minutes over high heat. Remove any scum. Remove from heat and drain well.

In a medium-size pot heat oil, sauté onions, garlic, and bell peppers, stirring for 5 minutes. Add the carrots and celery. Cook stirring for 5 minutes, then add the tomatoes, potatoes, 1 1/2 teaspoons salt, and the sugar. Stir for a couple of minutes, add beans, 2 1/2 cups of water, and mix well. Bring to a boil, reduce heat to simmer, cover, and cook for 40 minutes, stirring occasionally.

Remove pot from heat, let beans cool, and transfer beans to a shallow serving dish. Sprinkle with chopped parsley and serve with lemon quarters. Serve at room temperature.

Dried Broad Bean Puree

1 pound dried broad beans
2 medium-size onions, coarsely chopped
½ cup olive oil
1 teaspoon salt
½ tablespoon sugar
½ bunch fresh dill weed
Juice of ½ lemon

MAKES 5 TO 6 CUPS

**SERVES 6 TO 8 PEOPLE
AS A STARTER**

This is also used as stuffing for cooked artichoke bottoms (cut the recipe in half).

Place 6 cups of water in a 5-quart pot along with the beans, onions, ¼ cup plus table-spoons of the olive oil, salt, and sugar. Bring to boil, remove scum, cook on high heat for 10 minutes. Reduce heat to simmer, cover, and cook on low heat 45 minutes, stirring occasionally. Remove pot from the heat.

While the beans are cooking, separate dill stems from greens. Chop each separately.

With the back of a wooden spoon, force the bean mixture through a fine strainer into a bowl. Set aside 1 tablespoon of the dill weed greens, add the rest of the dill and the stems to the mixture, the lemon juice and 1 tablespoon of olive oil. Adjust salt if needed.

Rub a 6- to 8-cup glass bowl with 1 tablespoon of olive oil and sprinkle the reserved tablespoon of dill all around the bowl. Pour puree into the bowl. Let mixture cool to room temperature. Cover with foil and chill a least 6 to 7 hours in the refrigerator. Then before serving turn it upside down onto a flat plate and serve.

Eggplant Stuffed With Cheese

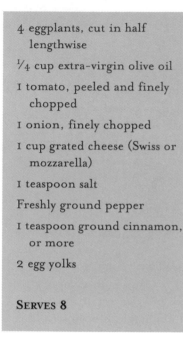

4 eggplants, cut in half lengthwise

¼ cup extra-virgin olive oil

1 tomato, peeled and finely chopped

1 onion, finely chopped

1 cup grated cheese (Swiss or mozzarella)

1 teaspoon salt

Freshly ground pepper

1 teaspoon ground cinnamon, or more

2 egg yolks

SERVES 8

This delightful recipe is from Gülden Sarıbaş and is from the Aegean province of Ayvalık.

*I*n a large pot boil 4 quarts salted water and place the unpeeled eggplants in the pot. Boil for 5 minutes or until they are cooked. Drain well and place on a baking sheet. Cut in half and using a spoon, gently remove the skin, set the skins aside in a baking dish, and mash the flesh.

Preheat oven to 360°F.

Heat the oil in a large skillet and sauté tomato and onion for 5 minutes. Add the eggplant flesh, grated cheese, salt, pepper and cinnamon to taste. Stir to mix well and cook 2 to 3 minutes, stirring, on medium heat.

Fill the reserved eggplant skins with the onion mixture. Beat 2 egg yolks and brush the tops of the filled eggplants with them. Bake eggplants for 20 minutes or until golden brown, or bake 15 minutes and place under the broiler until golden brown on top. Serve warm.

Fresh Fava Beans in Olive Oil

ZEYTİNYAĞLI BAKLA

2 pounds fresh fava beans

Juice of 1 lemon

1 tablespoon all-purpose flour

½ cup extra-virgin olive oil

1 medium onion, chopped fine

½ tablespoon sugar

Salt

1 cup chopped fresh dill

SERVES 6

Trim the ends from the fava beans and carefully cut away a very thin strip from each side seam (top to bottom) as this is bitter. Be careful not to cut the beans inside.

In a large bowl combine 2 cups water, the lemon juice, and flour. Place the beans in this paste as you cut them, swishing with your hand to mix. Set aside.

In a large pot heat the oil and sauté the onions, stirring, over medium heat for 3 minutes. Drain the fava beans saving 1 cup of the soaking liquid and add the beans, sugar, and salt to the onions, stirring to mix well. Cook, stirring frequently, for 3 minutes. Add the cup of the reserved soaking liquid and 1 cup of water. Stir to mix well and add ½ cup of the dill, mixing well.

Cut a circle of parchment paper to fit the pot and soak it with water. Press the paper over the top of the cooking beans and press lightly, then cover the pot, reduce the heat to medium-low and cook 30 to 35 minutes or until beans are tender. With a slotted spoon, remove beans to a bowl. If there is too much liquid left, bring to a boil and reduce to 5 or 6 tablespoons. Pour the liquid over beans. Sprinkle with the remaining ½ cup dill. Cool, cover, and refrigerate. Serve cold.

Vegetables

201

Fresh Peas With Carrots and Potatoes

ZEYTİNYAĞLI BEZELYE

1/2 cup extra-virgin olive oil

1 large carrot, diced in 1/4-inch cubes

1 large onion, finely chopped

1 large potato, peeled and diced in 1/4-inch cubes

5 to 6 stems dill, finely chopped

Salt

2 pounds fresh peas, shelled

1 teaspoon sugar

2 tablespoons dill weed, finely chopped

SERVES 4 AS A STARTER

In a large sauté pan heat the oil and sauté the onions, cooking and stirring for 3 to 6 minutes. Add the carrots, potatoes, and dill stems. Continue stirring and cooking for a couple of minutes more.

Add the peas and 2 1/2 cups of water, salt to taste, and sugar. Stir to mix well. Bring to a boil, reduce heat, and simmer on low heat for about 50 minutes. Remove pan from the heat and let it sit, covered, for 10 to 15 minutes.

Place mixture in a shallow serving dish and top with chopped dill.

Green Beans in Olive Oil

ZEYTİNYAĞLI FASULYE

You can also serve this as an appetizer.

2 pounds fresh string beans

½ cup extra-virgin olive oil

1 medium onion, finely chopped

2 large tomatoes, finely chopped

1½ teaspoons salt

1 teaspoon sugar

SERVES 6

Trim the ends off the beans and cut in half (lengthwise for French cut).

In a skillet, heat the oil over medium heat, add the onions, and sauté for 5 minutes. Then add the beans and sauté, stirring, for 3 to 4 minutes. Add the tomatoes and mix well. Add salt, sugar, and 1½ cups water, stirring to mix well.

Cut a piece of parchment paper in a circle to fit over the beans in the pot. Wet the paper and place on top the beans. Place the lid on the pot and cook for 10 minutes on high heat. Lower the heat to simmer and cook 25 to 30 minutes more. Check the beans to see if they are done. If all the water has been absorbed and the beans are still not cooked, add more hot water and cook until they are tender. When done remove the pot from the heat.

Serve at room temperature.

Green Beans
With Eggs and Garlic

YEŞİL FASULYELİ YUMURTA

2 pounds fresh string beans,
ends removed and cut into
½-inch pieces

1 stick butter

3 eggs

4 cloves garlic

1 to 2 teaspoons salt

SERVES 6

This recipe is from Bingöl-Yayla Dere in the eastern part of Turkey and is an old family recipe of Necla Akgül.

In a large pot cook beans, covered, in boiling salted water for a minute or two, then reduce heat and simmer for 15 to 20 minutes or until beans are tender. Remove from heat and drain well.

In a small skillet, melt the butter and when hot immediately crack and drop in the eggs, mixing well. As soon as eggs curdle, remove from heat.

Using a mortar and pestle, crush the garlic, salt, and 1 tablespoon water together. Set aside.

When beans are cool enough to handle, carefully squeeze by the handful to remove any excess water. Return beans to the pot along with the egg mixture and turn heat to medium. Stir in the garlic mixture, mixing well. Remove from heat and serve with bread.

Haricot Beans in Olive Oil

1 cup haricot or cannelloni beans

1½ teaspoons salt

⅓ cup extra-virgin olive oil

1 medium onion, finely chopped

3 cloves garlic

2 medium carrots, sliced in rounds crosswise

3 stalks celery, thinly sliced

2 medium tomatoes, peeled and chopped

1 teaspoon sugar

GARNISH:

2 tablespoon chopped parsley leaves

1 lemon, cut in 4 lengthwise pieces

SERVES 4 TO 5

Soak the beans overnight in water to cover.

Boil beans in 3 cups of water and ½ teaspoon of the salt for 10 minutes. Remove any scum. Remove from heat and drain well.

In a medium-size pot heat oil and sauté onions and garlic for 5 minutes. Add the carrots and celery, cook, stirring another 3 to 4 minutes. Add the tomatoes and continue stirring for a few minutes. Add 1 teaspoon salt, sugar, beans, and 2 cups of water. Bring to a boil, then reduce heat to a simmer. Check from time to time to see if the cooking liquid has been absorbed. If needed, add ½ cup of water. When cooking on low heat, the cooking time is 45 minutes or until tender.

Remove pot from heat and let cool. Transfer beans to a shallow dish and decorate with chopped parsley and lemon quarters. Eat at room temperature.

Vegetables

Okra Stew Aegean-Style

ZEYTİNYAĞLI BAMYA

¼ cup extra-virgin olive oil

1 large onion, finely chopped

4 to 5 cloves garlic, finely chopped

2 large tomatoes, peeled and chopped

Salt

1 pound frozen okra, thawed

Juice of ½ lemon

SERVES 4

This dish is eaten cold or at room temperature as a starter or light lunch dish.

In a saucepan heat the oil and sauté the onion and garlic for 6 to 7 minutes. Add tomatoes and salt to taste, mixing well, and cook, stirring, for 3 to 4 minutes. Add the okra and 1¼ cups water and salt to taste. Bring to a boil, cover, and simmer for 30 to 35 minutes.

Add the lemon juice, mix well, and cook for 2 to 3 minutes.

Omelet With Tomatoes

8 tablespoons butter

3 tablespoons vegetable oil

1 large onion, finely chopped

1 large green bell pepper, seeded, ribs removed, and finely chopped

1 small green chili pepper, finely chopped, optional

2 pounds fresh tomatoes, peeled, seeded, and chopped

3 eggs, lightly beaten

2 tablespoons finely chopped parsley, optional

SERVES 6 TO 8

This dish is eaten mostly in the summer when tomatoes are readily available.

*I*n a 4- or 5-quart pot heat the butter and oil over medium heat. Sauté the onions stirring, for 5 minutes. Add the peppers, stir to mix well, and cook, stirring occasionally for 15 to 20 minutes.

Add the tomatoes, stir well, cover, cook (stirring occasionally) over medium-low heat for 25 to 30 minutes or until vegetables are tender.

Add the eggs, stirring to mix, and let mixture cook for a minute until eggs curdle. Sprinkle with parsley, if desired, and serve.

Vegetables

Pinto Beans in Olive Oil

ZEYTİNYAĞLI BARBUNYA

2 pounds dried pinto beans

2 medium onions

2 large tomatoes, peeled, seeded, and chopped

¾ cup olive oil

2 ½ cups hot water

5 cloves garlic, chopped

½ to 1 teaspoon salt

1 teaspoon sugar

2 to 3 green chili peppers

SERVES 4 TO 6

This recipe needs to be started the day before serving.

Place the beans in 4 cups of cold water and soak overnight. Pour the liquid and beans into a large pot. Bring water to a boil, cover, reduce heat, and simmer the beans until partially tender.

Place the whole onions, tomatoes, and olive oil into a pot and cook over medium heat, stirring occasionally, until the tomatoes have softened. Add the hot water, garlic, salt, sugar, and cooked beans. Mix well, and place the whole green chili peppers on top. Cover and cook over low heat until the beans are tender and only the oil and a little liquid remains. A little more hot water can be added during the cooking process if needed. Remove the pan from the heat and set aside to cool with the lid still on. Arrange on a serving dish and place the peppers on top of the beans.

Red Lentil Köfte

²/₃ cup extra-virgin olive oil

1 large onion, finely chopped

1 tablespoon Red Bell Pepper
Paste (see page 37)*

Salt

Freshly ground pepper

1 teaspoon Aleppo pepper

1 cup dried red lentils, washed

1½ cups fine #1 bulgur

6 spring onions, whites and a
little green, sliced crosswise
in small pieces, optional

1 bunch fresh Italian parsley,
washed and finely chopped

SERVES 8 TO 10

An excellent vegetarian dish.

*H*eat the oil in a skillet and sauté the onions
for 8 to 10 minutes, stirring, on low-medium
heat until well cooked. Add the bell pepper
paste, Aleppo pepper, salt and pepper to taste.
Mix well and cook, stirring, for another 2
minutes. Remove from the heat and let rest.

Place the lentils in a 1-quart pot and cover
with 2 cups of cold water. Bring to a boil,
uncovered, reduce heat to medium and cook
for 20 to 25 minutes, stirring occasionally. If
and when white foam or scum appears, remove
it from time to time. When almost all the
water is absorbed, check the lentils and if they
are not cooked you can add a little more water
and continue cooking. When holes appear on
the surface and the lentils are cooked, add the
bulgur, mixing well, and turn off the heat.

Cover the pot and remove from the heat. Let the mixture rest for 10 minutes.
The bulgur will be cooked by the steam. Add the onion mixture, mix well with
a wooden spoon, cover, and let it rest again for 15 to 20 minutes.

Add half of the chopped spring onions and half of the chopped parsley to the
mixture, mixing well.

Using your hands, knead the mixture together for a few minutes and when
well blended take a tablespoon-size piece (from the mixture), roll into a ball,
and flatten into an oval shape (if desired you can wear rubber kitchen gloves
to do this). Repeat using all of the mixture, then place ovals in a serving dish
or on a platter, and sprinkle the remaining onions and parsley over the top.

Vegetables

Continued

*If you don't have Red Bell Pepper Paste, a tablespoon of tomato paste can be substituted.

Note: If the lentil and bulgur mixture is too hard, add a little boiling water and olive oil to soften. If too loose, add a little more bulgur. If you don't have time to shape the mixture, oil a round ring mold and place the lentil bulgur mixture in the mold, press it down gently, then turn it upside down on a round serving plate, unmold, and decorate the top with the rest of the chopped onions and parsley.

Spinach Stems With Rice

ZEYTİNYAĞLI PİRİNÇLİ ISPANAK KÖKÜ

1 pound fresh spinach stems

1 teaspoon salt

1 tablespoon all-purpose flour

½ cup extra-virgin olive oil

1 large onion, finely chopped

2 to 3 cloves garlic, finely chopped

2 tablespoons rice, washed

Juice of ½ lemon

SERVES 4 TO 6

Cut any dangling brown roots off the stems and trim the stems. Cut the stems into 1-inch pieces. Place the spinach stems in a large bowl of cold water mixed with salt (this makes the sand go to the bottom of the bowl). Swish, mixing stems and water, and let sit 10 to 15 minutes. Pour off the water, refill the bowl with cold water and let sit again without salt. Repeat two more times until there is no sand left. Place in a colander to drain well.

In a small bowl combine the flour and ¼ cup water to make a paste.

In a large skillet, heat the oil and sauté the onions and garlic, stirring for 5 minutes. Add the spinach stems and mix well. Add the rice and ½ cup water. Let mixture cook over low heat for 20 to 30 minutes until the rice is done. Add the lemon juice, mixing well, and then add the paste into the spinach and rice mixture, stirring constantly for 2 minutes. Remove from heat. It can be served warm or cold and can also be used as an appetizer.

The Imam Fainted

6 Italian eggplants,
   5 to 6 inches long

Salt

Vegetable oil for frying

3 medium onions

1/2 cup extra-virgin olive oil

3 cloves garlic, finely
   chopped

I cup chopped fresh Italian
   parsley

I teaspoon sugar

1/2 cup chopped canned
   tomatoes

I large tomato, sliced

I green bell pepper, seeded,
   ribs removed, sliced into
   1/2-inch strips

There is a story that tells of a famous Turkish priest or imam who was so delighted with his wife's eggplant creation that he fainted from pure pleasure. There are many versions of this dish. If possible prepare this a day or two ahead so the flavors can mellow.

Wash the eggplants and remove the leaves from around the stem, but leave the stem on. With a sharp knife, leaving a 1 1/2-inch border of peel at the tops and bottoms of the eggplants, remove the peel from the rest of the eggplants. Cut a thin slice off the bottoms of the eggplants so they are flat. With a small sharp knife make a deep slit lengthwise, from the top of the peeled area to the bottom of the peeled area, completely through the eggplants. Sprinkle the eggplants with salt and let them stand for 20 to 30 minutes. Rinse with cold water and dry them on a kitchen towel.

Place 2 to 3 inches of vegetable oil in a 5- to 6-quart pot or deep fryer and heat on high heat for about 10 minutes. Cook 2 to 4 eggplants at a time, depending on the size of the pot. Roll them frequently so they will lightly brown on all sides and cook evenly. Remove them from the oil when soft and let them drain in a fine sieve or colander. Cook remaining eggplants the same way. Lay the cooked eggplants in one or two large ovenproof skillets with the cut side up. Using a spoon, carefully open the slit to widen it.

Cut the onions in half and slice into very thin semicircles. Cut again in the opposite direction so thin strips are formed. Heat the olive oil and sauté the onions and garlic. Add the parsley, sugar, I to 2 teaspoons salt and canned tomatoes. Mix well. Stir and cook over high heat for 2 to 3 minutes. Open

GARNISH:
3 tablespoons chopped fresh
   Italian parsley

SERVES 6

the slits in the eggplants with a spoon while the eggplants are still hot and stuff the long slash of the eggplant. Press mixture down gently as you fill the eggplants.

Preheat oven to 400°F.

Pour 1 cup water around the sides of the eggplants in the pan. Garnish each eggplant with a slice of tomato and strip of bell pepper on top. Cover and cook over medium heat and bring to a boil. Place pan(s), uncovered, in the oven and cook for 30 minutes. Remove from oven, let cool and serve, or cover and chill. Garnish with parsley.

Zucchini Fritters

2 zucchinis, peeled and grated

3 spring onions, greens and whites finely chopped

6 sprigs fresh dill, finely chopped

5 to 6 sprigs fresh Italian parsley, finely chopped

6 to 7 sprigs fresh mint, finely chopped (or 1 teaspoon dried)

1/2 cup crumbled white Turkish cheese or feta cheese

3 eggs

1/4 cup plus 2 tablespoons all-purpose flour

Salt

Freshly ground pepper

3/4 cup vegetable oil for frying

MAKES 18

These can be served as a main course for vegetarians, or as a starter.

Squeeze the grated zucchini to remove any excess juice and place in a large bowl. Add the onions, dill, parsley, mint, cheese, eggs, flour, salt and pepper to taste to the zucchini. Stir to mix well.

Place the oil in a skillet and heat. Drop zucchini mixture by large tablespoonfuls into the hot oil and fry until golden brown on one side, then turn over and continue cooking until the other side is also golden brown. Before dropping each batch, stir the batter (this is a trick that insures the fritters won't be watery). Drain well on paper towels.

Zucchini With Rice

1 ½ pounds fresh zucchini

½ cup extra-virgin olive oil

1 large onion, finely chopped

2 cloves garlic, finely
   chopped

1 large bell pepper, seeded,
   cored, cut in quarters
   lengthwise and thinly sliced

2 large tomatoes, peeled and
   coarsely chopped

1 ½ tablespoons uncooked
   medium-grain white rice

Salt

GARNISH:

1 tablespoon finely chopped
   fresh dill

SERVES 4

This is a very light summer lunch dish or it can be a served on the side with any meat dish.

Wash and scrape the zucchini and cut in 4 lengthwise pieces, then cut crosswise (from the middle) making 8 pieces. Arrange zucchini in a saucepan side by side.

Heat oil in a skillet, add onions and garlic, sauté 6 to 7 minutes, add green pepper and tomatoes, and cook another 3 to 4 minutes. Remove the vegetables with a slotted spoon and add to the zucchini. If there is too much liquid left, bring to a boil and reduce to 5 or 6 tablespoons. Pour over the vegetables. Pour the sautéed vegetables over the zucchini, add rice, salt to taste, and 1 to 1 ¼ cups water. Bring to a boil, cover, and simmer 15 to 20 minutes.

Remove from heat and let it cool. It is eaten cold or room temperature. Top with finely chopped dill.

Jams and Jellies

Grapefruit or Orange Peel Jam

GREYFURT VE PORTAKAL KABUĞU REÇELİ

6 to 8 thick-skinned
   grapefruit or oranges

Sugar equal to peel weight

Juice of 1 lemon

MAKES 3 TO 4 CUPS

This is Nur's mother-in-law's recipe. When you grate the peel from the fruit, measure how much of it you have then mix it with an equal amount of sugar and store it in a jar. It can be used in cakes, or as a topping.

Save orange peels in a bag in the refrigerator every time you eat an orange or grapefruit and make the jam when you have a large quantity saved—they will keep for almost 3 weeks.

Carefully peel the skin off the fruits. Using a sharp, small knife, cut the peel in 4 sections from stem to bottom. Repeat until all the fruit is done. Squeeze the fruit to make 1 cup of fresh juice, cover and refrigerate.

Tightly roll up each peel. Using a straight threaded upholstery needle (use a long piece of cooking twine knotted at one end with a 2 inch tail), pass the needle and thread through a rolled peel starting at the rolled end or point. Repeat with each roll and push them next to one another along the string. Knot the thread at the other end when you are done so the rolls cannot slip off either end. Each roll should touch the one next to it.

Place the rolled peels in a pot and cover with enough cold water to cover and bring to a boil. Reduce heat to medium and cook until the peels are soft to the touch or a toothpick goes through easily, 30 to 45 minutes.

Drain the peels well and place them in cold water in a large bowl or pan. Let them sit for 1 hour, then change the water. Repeat two more times so the water is changed 3 times in 3 hours. This helps remove the bitterness from the fruit.

Drain the peels in a colander and press them with a clean kitchen towel to get rid of any excess water. Weigh the peels on a kitchen scale. You will need an equal amount of sugar. If you have a pound of cooked, drained peels you will need a pound of sugar.

Jams and Jellies

Continued

In a 3- or 4-quart pot, place the sugar, 1 cup of reserved fruit juice, and 1 cup of water. Place on high heat and bring to a boil, stirring and cooking until the sugar is dissolved. Reduce the heat to medium-high, add the string of peels, and cook for 1 hour. Remove any scum from the water as the peels cook.

Add the lemon juice and mix well. Cook for another 5 to 7 minutes. On a clean white plate, test the jam by dropping a little syrup from a spoon, a drop at a time, until the last drop holds its shape. Then the jam is done.

Remove the pot from the heat and let cool. Cut the string and place jam in several sterilized jars of any size. Turn upside down and let sit overnight before refrigerating.

Nur's Note: The jam jars are turned over so that the air in the jar disappears due to the weight of the jam, enabling it to last longer.

Orange Jam With Whole Fruit

5 navel oranges

5 cups sugar

Juice of 1 lemon

MAKES 3 TO 4 CUPS

Carefully grate the peel from the oranges and set aside. Place the oranges in a pot and cover with water. Bring to a boil, reduce heat to medium, and cook 15 minutes.

Drain the water off, add cold water to cover, and let oranges sit for an hour. Repeat two more times. This helps remove any bitterness from the fruit.

Cut the oranges in quarters, then cut the quarters in half and remove any seeds. Take the grated peel along with any seeds, and place in a small muslin bag.

Place the oranges in a 5-quart pot. Layer alternately oranges and sugar ending with the sugar. Add the lemon juice and shake the pot from side to side and in a circle to mix. Cook over medium heat, skimming off any scum that appears. Drop a little liquid from a spoon onto a white plate. If the last drop is firm and holds its shape jam is done.

Remove muslin bag, pour jam into sterilized jars of any size. Leave jars upside down over night then refrigerate.

Jams and Jellies

Peach Jam

2 pounds fresh peaches,
   peeled and cut into ½-inch
   slices or into small pieces

5 cups sugar

1 tablespoon lemon juice

MAKES 3 TO 4 CUPS

*I*n a 5-quart pot, layer the peaches and sugar, ending with a layer of sugar. Let sit 2 hours.

Place pot over medium heat and skim off any scum that appears. Do not stir. When it starts boiling then cook 10 to 15 minutes, then add the lemon juice and shake the pot from side to side and in a circle to mix. Cook another 4 to 5 minutes. Drop a little cooking liquid from a spoon onto a white plate. If the last drop is firm and holds its shape the jam is done.

Pour into sterilized jars of any size. Let jam sit overnight in jars, upside down then refrigerate.

Nur's Note: Shake the pan instead of stirring so you do not break the small pieces of fruit.

Prune Marmalade

2 pounds fresh ripe prune plums with the pits removed

2 ½ pounds (6 ¼ cups) sugar

Juice of 1 lemon

MAKES 3 TO 4 CUPS

Place the prunes in a pot with water to cover and cook over medium heat until prunes are tender. Push the prunes through a fine sieve or strainer with a wooden spoon. Skins should come off.

Take the remaining pulp and place it in a pot with the sugar. Mix well and cook over medium heat, stirring occasionally for 20 minutes. Stir in lemon juice, cook, stirring for another 5 minutes.

Take a little cooking liquid and drop it from a spoon onto a white plate. If the last drop is firm and holds its shape it is done. Pour into sterilized jars of any size, let jam sit overnight in the jars, then refrigerate.

Jams and Jellies

223

Quince Jam

2 pounds fresh quince
(4 or 5; usually available in
Korean markets)

5 cups sugar

1 tablespoon lemon juice

MAKES 3 TO 4 CUPS

This is a very popular jam. The slow simmering with peels and seeds will help the jam attain its deep rose color.

Wash the quince well and peel off thin skin layer using potato peeler. Save peel and seeds and place in a muslin bag. Section quince into 4 pieces lengthwise, each about 1 inch wide. Place the pieces of quince in a pot with water to cover, and simmer until tender, 15 to 20 minutes over low heat.

Add the sugar, stirring to mix well, and continue to cook over low heat. Add the muslin bag to the pot, cover the pot, and continue to simmer over very low heat for 30 minutes.

Add the lemon juice, stir to mix, and boil for 1 minute. Drop a little cooking liquid from a spoon onto a white plate. If the last drop is firm and holds its shape the jam is done. Remove the muslin bag and discard. Place in sterilized jars of any size, place them upside down overnight, and refrigerate.

Sour Cherry Preserves

1 pound black cherries or red
   sour cherries, washed and
   pitted

3 cups sugar

Juice of ½ lemon

MAKES 2 TO 2 ½ CUPS

*P*lace the cherries in a pot in layers, sprinkling each layer with sugar. Let the cherries and sugar layers sit for an hour, then place on high heat and bring to a boil. Reduce the heat to simmer and cook, uncovered, for about 30 minutes. Occasionally stir gently as the mixture cooks, and skim off any scum that rises to the top.

On a clean white plate test the jam by dropping a little syrup from a spoon, a drop at a time, until the last drop holds its shape. Then the jam is ready. Place in jars, turn them upside down overnight, then refrigerate.

Jams and Jellies

225

Strawberry Jam

2 pounds washed and hulled
fresh strawberries

2 pounds (5 cups) sugar

Juice of 1 lemon

MAKES 3 TO 4 CUPS

Pat the berries carefully on a paper towel to dry. In a 5-quart pot alternately make layers of the strawberries and sugar, ending with a layer of sugar. Let this sit for 2 hours so the berries will absorb some of the sugar.

Place the pot over medium heat. Skim off any scum that appears. When the jam begins to boil, add the lemon juice and gently shake it from side to side and in a circle. Do not stir. Cook for 30 minutes.

Drop a little cooking liquid from a spoon onto a white plate. If the last drop is firm and holds its shape, the jam is done. Place in sterilized jars of any size and leave jars upside down overnight, then refrigerate.

Turkish Dried Apricot Jam

I pound dried Turkish apricots
2 cups sugar
Juice of ½ lemon
MAKES 3 TO 4 CUPS

Soak apricots in cold water overnight. Remove apricots from the water using a slotted spoon and place the apricots in a pot with enough cold water to cover.

Over medium heat cook apricots for 40 to 45 minutes. Add the sugar and stir until dissolved, 5 to 10 minutes. Add lemon juice, stir, and cook another 5 to 10 minutes.

Test by dropping a few drops of cooking liquid from a spoon onto a small white plate. If the last drop from the spoon holds its shape and doesn't splatter, the jam is done. Place jam in sterilized jars of any size. Let them sit upside down overnight then refrigerate.

Jams and Jellies

Desserts

Almond Pudding With Pistachios

2/3 cup blanched almonds

3 tablespoons rice flour (available at Korean markets)

2 tablespoons cornstarch

4 cups milk

1 1/4 cups sugar

Pinch of salt

1 1/2 tablespoons grated coconut (dried)

GARNISH:
1/4 cup ground pistachio nuts

SERVES 10

Grind the almonds to a fine powder in a processor. Set aside.

Mix together the rice flour, cornstarch, and 3/4 cup of water. Mix well. Set aside.

Place the milk, sugar, and salt in a saucepan over medium heat, and whisking constantly in one direction, bring to a boil. Slowly add the rice flour mixture, continuing to whisk in one direction. Cook until the pudding begins to thicken, add the ground almonds and coconut, and continue whisking in one directions (which gives a better results).

Continue cooking another 10 to 15 minutes, until pudding is thick enough to coat a wooden spoon.

Pour the pudding in 10 (6-ounce) ramekins or cups and garnish with the ground pistachio nuts. Cool at room temperature, then refrigerate for at least 2 to 3 hours until serving.

Desserts

231

Baklava

SYRUP:

3 cups sugar

1 1/2 tablespoons lemon juice

2 cups clarified butter (page 9)

1 pound phyllo dough, thawed, at room temperature

3 cups coarsely chopped walnuts or pistachio nuts

MAKES ABOUT 2 1/2 DOZEN PIECES

Tomurcuk Erginay shared this recipe with us. Her mother taught it to her. It is quick, easy, delicious, and can be frozen.

Preheat oven to 300°F.

In a pot combine the sugar and 2 cups of water and bring mixture just to a boil. Stir in the lemon juice. Mix well. Lower heat to medium, cook, stirring, 8 or 9 minutes. Remove the pot from the heat and let cool. This can be made the night before and refrigerated.

In a pot heat the clarified butter.

Lay the phyllo on a cutting board and cut it in half forming sheets 13 by 8 1/2 inches. Place half of the cut phyllo dough into a 9 by 13-inch baking pan. If the phyllo does not fit perfectly, take a strip of aluminum foil, roll it up, and place in between the phyllo and the end of the pan, eliminating any space. The phyllo should touch both ends of the baking pan.

Spread all the nuts evenly over the top of the phyllo. Place the other half of the phyllo over the nuts. Using a sharp knife, cut diagonal lines 1 inch wide all the way to the bottom of the phyllo—right to the pan. Cut straight parallel lines 1 inch apart all the way through the phyllo. You will have diamond shaped pieces. Spoon all the butter, slowly, over the baklava, letting it absorb before adding more. Be sure and use all of the melted butter.

Bake the baklava for 35 to 45 minutes or until golden brown. Pour the cool syrup over the hot baklava and let it sit for a few minutes or chill and serve.

Bourma Dessert

2 1/2 cups sugar

1 teaspoon lemon juice

1 pound package phyllo dough, thawed, at room temperature

1 1/2 to 2 cups finely chopped walnuts

1 pound butter or margarine, melted and cooled

MAKES ABOUT 100 SMALL PIECES (OR YOU CAN MAKE BIGGER PIECES).

This dessert is very similar to Nightingale's Nests (page 241). Traditionally these are rolled in coils, but this version is easier and quicker.

Preheat oven to 400°F.

To prepare the syrup combine the sugar and 1 2/3 cup water in a saucepan, and cook, stirring over low heat until the sugar is dissolved. Boil gently for 5 minutes. Stir in the lemon juice, boil for a minute, then remove pan from the heat, and set aside.

Place a sheet of phyllo on a flat work surface with the shorter side nearest you. Place a long smooth rolling stick 1/4 inch wide and 15 inches long (a wooden dowel from the hardware store is fine) on the lower edge of the pastry. Fold 1 inch of the bottom edge of the phyllo over the stick. Sprinkle nuts along the entire length of the stick onto the phyllo sheet. Mist entire sheet lightly with water using a spray bottle.

Carefully, using your fingers, roll up the phyllo (like a jelly roll) enclosing the nuts. Roll until the whole sheet is rolled around the stick. Gently squeeze and push the rolled sheet gradually towards the center from both ends so it looks pleated (like an accordion, forming creases). Carefully remove the stick. Seal both ends by pinching with your fingers.

Place long strips of bourma seam-side down on an ungreased jelly roll pan (about 18 inches by 13 inches). Pour the melted butter over the long strips and bake for 15 to 20 minutes or until golden brown.

Remove the pan from the oven and pour the cold syrup over the hot pastry. Cut the bourma strips into smaller pieces, cover with aluminum foil, and cool.

Nur's Note: I especially cut it small for big parties so there are more pieces. Usually it is cut about 2 inches long.

Desserts

233

Dried Apricot Compote

30 dried apricots

I cup sugar

GARNISH:
1/2 cup slivered almonds

SERVES 6

Compotes are the lightest desserts in Turkish cuisine. Nur remembers every Ramadan when her grandmother used to prepare different compotes for her to eat at the end of the late night dinner before the fasting started at dawn. Dried prunes are done in exactly the same way.

Wash and soak the apricots in 6 cups of water overnight, or for at least 6 hours.

Place apricots and water in a saucepan and simmer, covered, for 20 to 25 minutes.

Add the sugar slowly, stirring until the sugar is dissolved and simmer for 4 to 5 minutes, uncovered. Remove pan from the heat and let cool to room temperature. Pour into 6 dessert dishes and chill until ready to serve. Garnish with nuts.

Dried Apricots Stuffed With Cream

KREMALI KURU KAYISI TATLISI

30 dried apricots

1⅓ cups sugar

1 cup whipping cream

⅓ cup finely ground pistachio nuts

GARNISH:
Chopped pistachio nuts, optional

SERVES 6

Soak the apricots overnight in 4 cups of cold water. Drain well and set aside.

Slice the apricots three-fourths of the way through for filling.

In a saucepan bring the sugar and 2 cups of water to a boil, mixing well. Reduce heat to simmer and cook for 5 minutes. Add the drained apricots and simmer, covered, for 10 to 15 minutes. Remove from heat, uncover, and let cool.

Whip the cream and place it in a pastry bag. Squeeze a little of the cream into the halved apricots and close the apricots. Dip the cream side in the ground nuts and place on a serving plate. Garnish with chopped pistachios if desired.

Figs Stuffed With Walnuts

20 dried figs

1 cup coarsely chopped walnuts

1 ½ cups sugar

GARNISH:

1 cup whipped cream

SERVES 5 TO 6

Soak the figs in warm water to cover for 20 minutes, drain well, and remove the stems. Using the handle of a wooden spoon, carefully poke a hole in the stem end and remove a little of the fig's inside. Carefully widen the hole with the spoon handle. Stuff the figs with the walnuts and place them side by side in a saucepan. Set aside.

In another saucepan heat 3 cups of water and the sugar and bring to a boil, mixing well to dissolve the sugar. Pour the mixture over the figs and cook on low heat until the syrup has been reduced to about a cup.

Place the figs and syrup in a shallow serving dish, cover, and refrigerate until serving. Serve cold with whipped cream.

Fried Doughnut Fritters in Syrup

LOKMA

SYRUP:

2 cups sugar

1 tablespoon fresh lemon juice

FRITTERS:

1/4 ounce dry yeast (1 packet)

1 1/2 cups lukewarm water

Pinch of sugar

2 cups all-purpose flour

1 tablespoon butter, melted and cooled to room temperature

1/2 teaspoon salt

Oil for frying

SERVES 6 TO 8

Prepare the syrup by combining the sugar and 1 1/2 cups water in a pot over medium heat. Stir well until sugar is dissolved, 5 to 10 minutes. Stir in lemon juice, return to a boil, and remove pot from heat. Let syrup cool.

Dissolve the yeast in the warm water with the sugar and mix well. Let mixture sit 10 minutes or until it begins to foam.

Place the flour in a large bowl and make a well in the center. Place the butter, salt, and yeast mixture in the well, and mix with the flour. Mix into a batter using a wooden spoon or the dough hook or paddle beater on your mixer. Cover the bowl and let mixture rise for an hour or until double in bulk.

Heat the oil to 350°F in a deep pot or electric fryer. Grab a handful of dough and squeeze your hand into a loose fist. Using an oiled teaspoon, remove the dough that comes out of the circular opening between your thumb and first finger. This should be about an inch in diameter. Don't worry about the shape. They are good no matter what they look like. Each time before using spooning off more dough, dip the spoon into a glass of water. This makes it easier to drop the dough off.

Drop batter into the hot oil. Do not crowd the pan. They should rise to the surface as soon as you drop them into the hot oil. Stir carefully to ensure that they brown on all sides. You do not want them to brown too quickly, so adjust heat if necessary. Repeat using all the batter. Drain well on paper towels. Drop them into the syrup for a minute. If you like them sweeter, let them sit in the syrup for a few minutes.

Desserts

Lady's Navel

SYRUP:

2 cups sugar

2 teaspoons fresh lemon juice
(save the quarter piece of
lemon used)

DOUGH:

7 tablespoons butter

1 teaspoon salt

1½ cups flour, sifted

3 eggs, at room temperature

8 cups vegetable oil

GARNISH (OPTIONAL):

Chopped pistachio nuts

Whipped or clotted cream

SERVES 8 TO 10

Prepare the syrup by placing the sugar, 1¾ cups water, lemon juice, and the quarter piece of lemon in a pot. Cook over medium heat, stirring constantly to dissolve the sugar. When the sugar has dissolved, bring to a boil, reduce heat to simmer, and cook, uncovered, for 10 minutes. Remove pot from the heat and let cool.

Make the dough: In a 3-quart pot, place 1¾ cups water, the butter, and salt. Bring to a boil, mixing well. Reduce the heat to low and slowly add the flour stirring constantly with a wooden spoon until you have a smooth thick dough that resembles mashed potatoes, 5 to 6 minutes. Remove from the heat and let the dough cool, then add the eggs, one at a time, beating well after each addition until well blended and no lumps remain. Cover with a damp cloth and refrigerate for 30 minutes.

Place the oil in a large fry pan and heat it, then remove it from the heat. Oil your hands frequently or you will not be able to shape the dough. Take a walnut-size piece of dough and roll it between your hands into a ball. Repeat using all the dough. Flatten each ball slightly and by pressing with one finger, make an indentation in the center of each ball to form a hollow spot.

Toss about 20 cookies into the pan and place the pan back on the stove and begin cooking over low heat. It is very important that the oil not be hotter than lukewarm at this time so the pastry will puff up properly. Do not crowd them in the pan. As they fry they will puff up and slowly rise to the surface in about 5 minutes. Increase the heat to medium and continue cooking, stirring constantly until the navels are golden brown on all sides. They need to cook slowly so this will take 10 to 15 minutes. Remove from the pan with a slotted spoon and drain well on paper towels.

Do not forget to cool the oil to lukewarm every time it is removed from the heat and a new batch is prepared. Some cooks prefer to use 2 pans and eliminate the waiting.

Place the drained navels in a large bowl or pan and pour the cooled syrup over them. The longer they sit in the cold syrup the sweeter they get! Traditionally, they are left for 2 hours. Let them sit 20 to 30 minutes, stirring occasionally to make sure all sides are saturated. Remove them and place them on a serving dish. If desired sprinkle with ground pistachio nuts and serve with clotted cream or whipped cream.

Variation: For Veizer's Fingers (Vezir Parmaği), instead of shaping the dough into balls, Place some of the dough into a large pastry bag fitted with a crown shaped tip that is ½-inch across. Pipe out pieces that are 1½-inches long onto a lightly greased pan (or directly into the pan of oil). Follow the rest of the recipe exactly as the Lady's Navels.

Mastic Pudding in Rose Syrup

SU MUHALLEBİSİ

2 to 3 pieces mastic

I teaspoon sugar

7½ heaping tablespoonfuls cornstarch

3½ cups milk

SYRUP:

4 cups sugar

¼ cup rose water

GARNISH:

Sliced or whole peeled pistachio nuts and peeled slivered almonds

SERVES 10 (MAKES 10 INDIVIDUAL RAMEKINS OF 6 OUNCES EACH)

This is a specialty from Gaziantep in the southeast part of Turkey. You can purchase mastic and rose water from Greek or Mediterranean markets.

Using a mortar and pestle crush mastic and sugar into a powder.

In a saucepan over medium heat, combine cornstarch, cold milk, and ½ cup water, stirring constantly. Add the mastic and sugar, reduce heat to low-medium, and cook, whisking constantly until the pudding becomes thick.

Run a 9 by 13-inch baking pan or 10 (½-cup) ramekins or Pyrex bowls under cold water, then pour the water out. Pour in the pudding.

Prepare the syrup. Place the sugar and 4 cups of water in a saucepan and bring to a boil, stirring until the sugar is dissolved. Reduce heat to medium and cook, uncovered, for 40 minutes. Let cool and chill.

Add rose water to the syrup right before serving, mixing well. Place the syrup in a large serving bowl, cut pudding into small ½-inch squares and soak them in the syrup. Pudding and syrup may be spooned into individual desert bowls or ramekins if desired. Garnish with nuts before serving.

Nur's Note: all starches should be added to a cold liquid (water, milk) and then stirred into the recipe.

Nightingale's Nest

2 ½ cups sugar

1 tablespoon fresh lemon
juice

1 pound phyllo dough, thawed,
at room temperature

1 cup finely chopped walnuts

2 sticks sweet cream butter,
melted and cooled

½ cup chopped pistachio
nuts

MAKES 26 LARGE NESTS

Preheat oven to 375°F.

To prepare the syrup combine the sugar and 1 ¼ cups water in a saucepan, and cook, stirring over low heat until the sugar is dissolved. Boil gently for 5 minutes. Stir in the lemon juice, boil for 1 minute, then remove pan from the heat and set aside and chill.

Cut the phyllo sheets in half so each sheet is 13 by 8 ½ inches. Using one sheet at a time, fold or drape 1 inch of the phyllo over a ¼-inch-thick stick or dowel, and sprinkle nuts along the entire length of the sheet (along the stick end). Using a spray bottle, lightly mist the entire sheet with water so the phyllo will not dry out while baking.

Using your fingers, carefully push the stick with the phyllo draped over it, over the nuts, roll up the remaining phyllo. Leave an inch of phyllo unrolled at the end. With your fingers, push the rolled phyllo towards the center of the stick from the end, pleating or crinkling it a little. Carefully remove the stick and bring the ends together making sure the unrolled inch of phyllo is in the center of the circle you are forming. This makes the nest.

Carefully pour the melted butter over all the nests. Place nests on an ungreased jelly roll pan and bake for 15 to 18 minutes or until golden brown.

After baking, pour cold syrup over hot nests and sprinkle chopped pistachio nuts into the center of each nest.

Desserts

Noah's Pudding

¾ cups shelled wheat (available in health food or Middle Eastern stores)

2 tablespoons uncooked extra-long-grain white rice

1 tablespoon grated orange peel

¼ cup canned garbanzo beans (chickpeas), washed, drained, and skins removed

¼ cup canned cannellini beans, washed and drained

½ cup raisins

1 cup sugar

½ cup milk

2 tablespoons rose water

½ cup dried apricots, cut into quarters

8 dried figs, cut into quarters

GARNISH:
Walnut halves

Whole blanched almonds

Pine nuts

Currants

Chopped pistachios

1 teaspoon ground cinnamon

SERVES 8

It is said that this pudding was prepared on the ark to celebrate the day the flood waters subsided and Noah and his family could finally leave the ark. Before leaving the ark they took all the remaining foodstuffs and made them into a sweet soup. To commemorate this last meal a similar dessert is prepared and shared with others.

This recipe must be prepared two days before serving.

Soak the wheat and rice overnight in water to cover, then drain well.

In a large pot place the drained wheat and rice with 12 cups of water. Bring to a boil, reduce heat to simmer, stirring occasionally, partially cover, and cook until the grains are tender, about 60 minutes.

Add the orange peel, chickpeas, beans, and raisins. Simmer for 10 minutes more then add the sugar, stirring and mixing well. Continue simmering for 10 minutes, stirring occasionally. Bring to a boil, add the milk, and cook for 15 minutes more. Turn off the heat and stir in the rose water. The mixture is not thick like a pudding. If it is thick you can add some more hot water and boil for a couple of minutes.

In the bottom of a 13 by 9-inch Pyrex pan or individual serving bowls, place the apricots and figs. Carefully spoon the pudding over the fruit. Let it rest until cool, then cover and refrigerate overnight. Decorate the top with nuts, currants, pistachios, and cinnamon.

Orange Baklava
à la Kazan

SYRUP:

3 cups sugar

Juice of 1 or 2 lemons

BAKLAVA:

4 large oranges

2 ½ to 3 cups sugar (1 pound)

1 pound phyllo dough, thawed and at room temperature

1 pound unsalted butter, clarified (page 9)

GARNISH (OPTIONAL):

Whipped cream

Mint leaves

MAKES 24

Kazan is a special chafing dish used long ago to prepare food for the sultan. It is also the name of a very well known Washington, D.C. area Turkish restaurant owned by Zeynel Uzun. This dessert was first prepared in 1973 by Zeynel in an Istanbul restaurant Konyalı (where he worked) for her majesty Queen Elizabeth II and served to her at Topkapı Palace. She loved it and so will you!

Make the syrup: Place the sugar and 2 cups of water in a saucepan and bring to a boil, stirring until the sugar is dissolved. Reduce heat to medium and cook syrup, uncovered, for 10 to 15 minutes. Stir in lemon juice, mix well, and cook another minute or two. Remove from heat, let cool, then refrigerate.

Using a small sharp knife, slice the peel from the tops and bottom of the oranges, then slice the orange peel in 6 pieces (from top to bottom), leaving the orange intact. Place the peel in a large pot with cold water to cover and bring to a boil. Reduce heat and cook for 15 minutes. Place the peel in a colander to drain. Place peel in a bowl of cold water and let sit until cool, then drain. Do this step twice. This helps remove any bitterness from the peel. Drain well, pressing with a clean kitchen towel to get rid of excess water. Place the peel in a food processor and chop.

Slice the oranges into ½-inch slices and cut again into ½-inch pieces. Place the pieces of orange in a large bowl with the sugar and chopped peel. Mix well and let the mixture sit for an hour. This allows the pieces of orange to absorb some of the sugar. Place the orange-sugar mixture in a pot and cook 15 to 20 minutes on low heat, stirring constantly. Remove from the heat and let cool. If there is a large amount of liquid, drain it and discard. Consistency should be like a paste. This can be made ahead in large batches and stored in the refrigerator.

Desserts

C o n t i n u e d

Place a sheet of phyllo on a work surface, covering the rest of the phyllo with a very slightly damp- ened towel to keep it from drying out. Brush the sheet lightly with the melted butter and fold the sheet in half to form a sheet approximately 13 by 8-inches. Turn the phyllo so the long edge is fac- ing you and spread about a teaspoon of filling across the top, about 1 ½ inches from the edge. Brush the phyllo below the row of filling lightly with melted butter, bring the long edge over the filling, and continue to roll the phyllo up like a log or jelly roll. Carefully begin to coil one end of the log, continuing until you have a "rose." Place on a lightly greased jelly roll pan and gently press down on the top of the rose with your fin- gers. Brush the top and sides of the rose with a little melted butter. Repeat, making and coiling the remaining baklavas.

Preheat the oven to 350°F.

Bake the baklava for 15 to 25 minutes, until light- ly browned. Check and make sure the bottoms are lightly brown also. This is very important.

Remove baklavas from the oven and carefully pour the chilled syrup over each rose. Serve with a dab of whipped cream topped with a mint leaf on top, if desired.

Zeynel's Note: Either the syrup must be cold and the baklava warm or hot, or the baklava must be cold and the syrup hot. If both are the same temperature the dessert will get mushy.

Taste of Turkish Cuisine

Pistachio Squares

SYRUP:

3 cups sugar

3 tablespoons lemon juice

CAKE:

7 eggs, separated

2/3 cup sugar

Pinch of salt

1/2 cup all-purpose flour, sifted

2 1/2 cups unsalted pistachio nuts, ground fine in a food processor

1/3 cup butter, melted and cooled

GARNISH:

1/3 cup chopped pistachio nuts

Whipped cream, optional

SERVES 10 TO 12

Preheat oven to 350°F.

Prepare the syrup by boiling the sugar, 2 1/2 cups water, and lemon juice together for 10 minutes, stirring occasionally. Remove from heat and chill.

Place the egg yolks in a mixing bowl with the sugar and beat until light in color and well blended, about 5 minutes. In a separate bowl beat the egg whites with a pinch of salt until they are stiff but not glossy like meringue. Set aside. Gradually add the flour, ground nuts, and butter to the yolk mixture. Slowly fold in the beaten egg whites, one half at a time.

Grease and lightly flour an 8-inch springform pan and pour in the pistachio mixture. Sprinkle the chopped pistachio nuts over the top and bake for 35 to 40 minutes, or until a toothpick inserted in the middle comes out clean.

Pour or ladle the cooled syrup over the cake a little at a time, let it absorb, and repeat until all the syrup is used. Let the dessert sit at room temperature for 2 hours. Cut into squares, and if desired, serve with whipped cream.

Desserts

Quince Compote

3 large quinces, peeled and
 cut into thin slices

²⁄₃ cup sugar

SERVES 4 TO 6

The quince looks like a pear and smells somewhat like a pineapple. Autumn is the season for quinces. Store them away from other fruits until they become soft and juicy and release their wonderful aroma. The fruit turns pink when cooked.

When someone doesn't feel well or has an upset stomach, instead of getting Jell-O or something else that's light, in Turkey a mom makes this compote.

Place 3 cups of water and the sliced quinces in a 3-quart pot. Bring to a boil, reduce heat to simmer, cover, and cook for 30 minutes. Add the sugar, mix well, cover and continue cooking for another 15 minutes or until quinces are tender.

Pour quinces and cooking liquid into a serving bowl and chill.

Quince Dessert

7 quinces

Juice of 1 small lemon

2 ¾ cups sugar

4 whole cloves

GARNISH:

1 cup whipped cream,
   optional

¼ cup chopped pistachio
   nuts

SERVES 7

Nur introduced me to quince and am I sorry it took so long to discover this fabulous fruit.

Peel the quinces and cut the quinces in half and remove the seeds, saving the peel and seeds from 2 quinces.

In a large 4-quart pot or pan place the quinces with the peel and seeds. Pour in 4 cups of water and the lemon juice. Cover and cook over medium heat for 15 minutes or until soft. Pour sugar and cloves over the quinces and cook, uncovered, shaking the pan from side to side to help dissolve the sugar. Cook 30 to 40 minutes. Remove from heat, turn quinces over and let cool. Chill, turn quinces over again so the cored part is up until ready to serve. Quinces will change to a pinkish color.

Serve with whipped cream and chopped pistachio nuts, if desired.

Nur's Note: Don't add the sugar at the beginning as it hardens the fruit.

Raisin Compote

½ cup sun-dried raisins

¾ cup sugar

2 sticks cinnamon

8 whole cloves

SERVES 3 TO 4

Soak the raisins in warm water to cover for 30 to 45 minutes. Drain well.

In a saucepan bring the sugar, 2½ cups water, cinnamon sticks, and cloves to a boil, stirring to dissolve the sugar. When the sugar is dissolved, reduce heat to simmer, add the raisins, cover, and cook for 8 to 10 minutes.

Rice Dessert in Syrup

SYRUP:

4 ¾ cups sugar

I teaspoon fresh lemon juice

RICE:

1 ¼ cups uncooked Turkish
(Baldo) rice or medium-
grain or white Arborio rice

I quart milk

2 ½ sticks sweet cream butter,
at room temperature

3 eggs

I teaspoon baking powder

½ teaspoon mastic (available
in Greek or Mediterranean
markets)

I teaspoon vanilla extract

GARNISH:

⅓ cup chopped pistachio
nuts

SERVES 12 OR MORE

This recipe is from an old family friend who was from the European part of Turkey.

Soak the rice in cold water for 20 minutes.

Make the syrup: In a large pot place the sugar and 3 cups of water. Bring to a boil and cook, stirring occasionally, for 15 minutes. Add lemon juice, cook for another minute, mix well, remove from the heat and let cool.

Using your hands, try and break up the rice grains. Drain the rice and place the rice and the milk in a large saucepan and cook over low heat until all the milk is absorbed. Stir constantly so the milk and rice will not stick to the pan and burn. It should take 20 to 25 minutes for the milk to be absorbed.

Gradually add large chunks of butter and continue cooking on low heat for 20 minutes. Remove the pan from the heat and let rice cool.

Preheat the oven to 400°F. Grease a 13 by 18-inch jelly roll pan. Beat the eggs and pour into the cooled rice. Mix well. Add the baking powder, mastic, and vanilla, mixing well. Pour rice into greased pan, and smooth the top with a knife.

Cut the rice into 2-inch squares and bake for 30 to 35 minutes or until the top is golden brown. Remove from the oven and pour the cold syrup over the rice squares.

Garnish with chopped pistachio nuts.

Desserts

Rice Pudding

½ cup uncooked medium-grain white rice

2 to 3 pieces mastic (available in Greek or Mediterranean markets)

I cup plus I teaspoon sugar

I quart milk

2 teaspoons vanilla extract

2 heaping tablespoons corn-starch

2 egg yolks

SERVES 8 TO 10

Using the right rice size is important for the success of this recipe.

Place the rice and 2 cups water in a 3-quart pot. Stir and cook over medium heat until all the water is absorbed (about 30 minutes), stirring frequently.

Crush the mastic and I teaspoon of the sugar together using a small mortar and pestle. Stir in the milk, I cup sugar, vanilla, and mastic mixture and continue cooking, stirring frequently, over medium heat for 10 minutes.

In a bowl dissolve the cornstarch in ¼ cup of water, then add the egg yolks and mix well. Whisking constantly, slowly pour the cornstarch mixture into the milk mixture, and cook until large bubbles begin to appear and mixture has thickened (this does not take very long). Quickly remove the pot from the heat and pour the pudding into individual ramekins or into a serving bowl.

If desired, ramekins or serving bowl can be placed under a preheated broiler just until the tops begin to brown. Refrigerate 3 hours or overnight until well chilled.

Nur's Note: If the mixture is too loose for some reason, add a little more cornstarch mixed in water.

Saffron Pudding

⅓ cup uncooked short-grain white rice

½ teaspoon saffron

½ cup boiling water

1 cup sugar

¼ cup rose water

3 tablespoons arrowroot

GARNISH (OPTIONAL):
6 teaspoons pine nuts

3 teaspoons currants

6 teaspoons chopped pistachios

SERVES 6

This dessert is traditionally served at weddings and on religious holidays.

Place the rice and 4 cups of water in a 3-quart pot and bring to a boil. Reduce heat, cover, and cook for 20 to 25 minutes or until rice is tender.

In a small bowl mix the saffron with ¼ cup boiling water. Add the sugar, saffron mixture, and rose water to the rice, whisking to mix well. Turn the heat up and boil for a minute, whisking constantly. Reduce heat to medium.

Whisk together the remaining ¼ cup boiling water and the arrowroot. Whisk into the rice mixture and cook, whisking for 2 to 3 minutes. Remove from the heat and pour into serving glasses or bowls.

Cool to room temperature and then chill until serving. If desired, garnish with the pine nuts, currants, and pistachio nuts.

Semolina Cake With Syrup

CAKE:

1 cup fine-grain semolina

1 cup all-purpose flour, sifted

1 tablespoon baking powder

1 cup sugar

4 eggs, at room temperature

3/4 cup plain yogurt

4 1/2 tablespoons butter, melted and cooled

Grated peel of 1 lemon

SYRUP:

3 cups sugar

3 teaspoons fresh lemon juice

GARNISH:

2 to 3 tablespoons finely chopped pistachio nuts

SERVES 12

This cake should be made the day before serving.

Preheat oven to 350°F. Grease and flour a 10-inch springform pan.

In a large mixing bowl mix together the semolina, flour, baking powder, sugar, eggs, yogurt, butter, and lemon peel for 5 minutes at medium speed.

Pour the batter in the prepared pan and bake for 30 to 35 minutes.

Place the syrup ingredients and $3\frac{1}{3}$ cups water in a 3-quart pot. Fifteen minutes before the cake has finished baking, prepare the syrup. Boil the sugar, water, and lemon juice, stirring. Reduce heat to simmer and cook 10 minutes.

Remove the cake from the oven and carefully spoon the hot syrup over the cake. You may want to poke holes in the cake with a fork or toothpick so the syrup can really be absorbed. Cool to room temperature for 5 to 6 hours. Decorate by sprinkling the top with chopped pistachio nuts. Cover and refrigerate until serving.

Nur's Note: When the lemon juice is added after the syrup has cooked it makes a thinner syrup.

Semolina Helva

1 ½ cups butter

3 tablespoons pine nuts

3 ½ cups coarse semolina

2 ½ cups milk

2 ½ cups sugar

Ground cinnamon

SERVES 10

Traditionally this is served after a funeral. After late afternoon prayers this is served with lemonade to guests and family members who came to offer condolences and pray. It is also served on the anniversary of the death of a close relative to remember them and pray for their souls. It is shared with friends.

In a 4-quart saucepan melt the butter, stir in the nuts, and cook until the nuts begin to change color. Stir in the semolina and cook over a very low heat, stirring constantly with a wooden spoon for 40 to 45 minutes. There will be only a slight color change. Do not overcook or the taste will be spoiled.

Place the milk, sugar, and 2 ¼ cups water in another saucepan and bring to a boil over medium heat, stirring constantly with a wooden spoon. Gradually pour the boiling milk mixture over the semolina, and stirring in the same direction, lower the heat and cook and stir for about 3 minutes or until all the liquid has been absorbed and mixture is very thick.

Remove the pan from the heat, cover with 2 paper towels, cover with the lid of the pan, and set aside for 30 minutes. Do not touch it.

Place semolina in a serving dish and sprinkle with cinnamon.

Serve warm or cold.

Desserts

Shredded Phyllo With Walnuts

CEVİZLİ TEL KADAYIF

SYRUP:

2 1/2 cups sugar

1 tablespoon lemon juice

1 pound shredded phyllo
dough, thawed, at room
temperature

1 1/4 cups unsalted butter

2 cups coarsely chopped
walnuts

GARNISH (OPTIONAL):

2 cups whipped cream

Chopped pistachio nuts

MAKES 15 SQUARES

Make the syrup: Combine the sugar and 2 1/4 cups water in a 3-quart saucepan. Bring to a boil and boil for 5 minutes, stirring until the sugar dissolves. Reduce heat and simmer, uncovered, for 10 to 15 minutes. Stir in the lemon juice, remove pan from the heat, and set aside.

Preheat oven to 375°F. Butter a 13-inch by 9-inch baking pan.

Separate the shredded phyllo dough into 2 equal piles.

In a large bowl combine 1/4 cup of the melted butter with half of the shredded phyllo dough. Press this mixture down on the bottom of the prepared pan. Sprinkle the walnuts evenly over the butter phyllo layer. Combine the remaining phyllo with 1/4 cup of melted butter and carefully press on top of the walnuts. Pour the remaining melted butter over the top of the dessert and bake for 35 minutes.

Carefully place a same size baking pan over the top of the dessert and flip it over into the new pan and continue baking for another 25 minutes. This will prevent the bottom from burning.

Spoon the hot syrup (reheat if necessary) over the hot pastry and return to the oven for 5 minutes. Remove from the oven and set aside to cool.

Garnish with whipped cream and nuts, if desired.

Sweet Rounds With Almonds

SYRUP:

3 cups sugar

1 tablespoon fresh lemon juice

COOKIES:

1 cup confectioners' sugar

1 cup butter, softened to room temperature

2 eggs

3 cups all-purpose flour plus 1 tablespoon (more may be needed)

1 teaspoon baking soda

1 teaspoon vanilla extract

60 whole blanched almonds

MAKES 60 PIECES

The first time I met Nur she served these cookies. I ate at least eight of them. A few days later I realized I wanted the recipe, but could not remember the exact name of this particular cookie since she had served such a variety. All I could remember was that the name sounded like Shakespeare, so that's what I called them. Luckily she understood which recipe I wanted and sent it to me (seker is pronounced "shaker" in Turkish). I still call them Shakespeares though!

In a 3-quart pot, stir together the sugar, 3 cups water, and lemon juice, stirring until it begins to boil and sugar is dissolved. Reduce heat to simmer and cook another 10 minutes. Remove from the heat and let cool.

In a large bowl, using your fingers, mix together the confectioners' sugar, butter, and eggs. Add the flour, baking soda, and vanilla working until dough is formed. It will feel greasy to the touch. Roll dough around on a lightly floured surface until you have a smooth ball.

Preheat oven to 350°F.

Pinch off a walnut-size piece of dough, roll it between your palms until it is round and smooth. Place on an ungreased jelly roll pan. Repeat using all the dough. Place an almond, point side down, in the center of each cookie. Bake for 30 minutes until lightly golden brown. Do not let the cookies burn, check the bottoms after 25 minutes.

Remove cookies from the oven and spoon the cool syrup over them. Let them sit in the syrup for 15 minutes then turn them over and let them sit some more. The longer they sit, the more syrup they absorb, and the sweeter they get! These can be frozen.

Desserts

255

Walnut-Stuffed Cookies in Syrup

SYRUP:

2 cups sugar

Juice of ¼ lemon

COOKIES:

½ cup vegetable oil

1½ cups milk

½ tablespoon baking powder

2 cups all-purpose flour

½ cup walnut halves

MAKES 22 TO 24 COOKIES

This is a wonderful inexpensive dessert that has no eggs. Some people use a mold to shape these cookies, others press them against the wire mesh of a sieve, a colander, or grater. The idea is to end up with a slightly raised design on the cookies.

Prepare syrup by boiling the sugar, 2 cups water, and lemon juice, stirring to dissolve the sugar. Reduce heat to simmer and cook for 20 minutes. Remove from heat and let cool.

In a large bowl combine the oil, milk, and baking powder. Add the flour and mix together to form dough. If needed, add a little more flour. Dough should feel a little oily.

Preheat oven to 400°F.

Oil a mold, sieve, or the sunburst shape on a plastic grater. If you don't have any of these, you can make a design with the tines of a fork.

Divide the dough into golf-ball-size pieces and press on the oiled mold or roll between your palms and flatten into a 2-inch circle.

Remove dough from the mold and press a walnut half into the center of the flat side. Bring the sides together to enclose the nut. Pinch well to seal. The cookie should resemble an oval cocoon with a raised design all around.

Place the cookie on an ungreased jelly roll pan and bake for 20 minutes. Cookies should be lightly golden brown. Turn oven up to 425°F and bake another 5 to 10 minutes.

When cookies are cool enough to handle pour the warm syrup over them and roll them around in the syrup. Let them sit in the syrup overnight to absorb it, turning them frequently if possible.

Drinks

Cool Yogurt Drink

I cup plain yogurt

I to I ½ cups ice water
(depends if you like it thin
or thick)

Pinch of salt

SERVES 2

This refreshing beverage is especially good on hot days.

Place the yogurt and ice water in a blender.
Add the salt and beat for a minute or two.
Pour the mixture into a pitcher or container
and refrigerate until ready to use.

Drinks

259

Grandma's Lemonade With Mint

Fresh mint leaves (start with a bunch)

1 cup sugar

Juice of 5 medium-size lemons

SERVES 5

If this is too sweet for your sweet tooth, add an extra cup of water.

Remove the leaves from the mint stems. Wash the mint leaves and press them down into a 1/2-cup measure. You should have enough leaves to fill the cup.

Place the mint leaves, sugar, and lemon juice in a blender and blend. Strain the mint mixture through a fine sieve and place in a large pitcher. Add 2 1/2 cups of cold water, taste, and if too sweet add more water. Add ice if desired. Stir well.

Chill and serve in glasses garnished with additional mint leaves or a slice of lemon.

Turkish Coffee

1 ½ teaspoons pulverized
Turkish ground coffee

1 teaspoon sugar

SERVES 1

This drink is served by street vendors, restaurants, sidewalk cafes, and in all homes. One has to have an acquired taste for this black, heavy drink, though. It is usually prepared in a special pot called cezve. It has been a symbol of hospitality since it was introduced from Yemen in the sixteenth century during the reign of Suleyman the Magnificent. Europe's fascination for coffee grew from their direct contacts with the Ottoman Turks. The Turkish expression, "the memory of a single cup of coffee lasts 40 years," reflects this sentiment of peace, friendship, love, and respect. Turkish coffee is always taken leisurely in small sips and from small cups. "Afiyet olsun!"

This recipe is for medium-sweet coffee. I drink my coffee without any sugar, called sade kahve (plain coffee). The amount of sugar is up to your taste. It can be less or more.

For each person place 1 demitasse cupful of cold water into a jezvah (or saucepan with a pouring spout) and add the Turkish coffee and sugar. Stir to mix well. Place the pot over low heat, stirring until the sugar has dissolved. Cook to a rising boil and immediately remove from the heat. Pour or spoon the forth evenly into the tiny cups and replace the pot on the heat. When the coffee begins to rise remove the pot and fill the cups.

Serve immediately.

Bibliography

Algar, Alya. *Classical Turkish Cooking*. New York: HaperCollins, 1991.

Eren, Neşet. *The Art of Turkish Cooking*. New York: Hippocrene Books, 1993.

Index

A

Albanian Liver with Onion Relish, 115
Ali Pasha Pilaf, 177
Almond Pudding with Pistachios, 231
Appetizers
    Black Sea Cornmeal Cooked with
      Cheese, 19
    Cabbage Leaves Stuffed with
      Rice, 20
    Carrots with Garlic and Yogurt,
      22
    Drained Yogurt, 42
    Eggplant Salad with Olive Oil, 23
    Eggplant Salad with Yogurt, 24
    Eggplant with Tahini, 25
    Fried Eggplant, 26
    Fried Zucchini, 27
    Grape Leaves Stuffed with Rice, 28
    Hot Olive Balls with Cheese
      Pastry, 30
    Hummus, 31
    Jerusalem Artichokes with
      Vegetables, 32
    Leeks, Carrots, and Rice in
      Olive Oil, 33
    Lemon Sauce, 34
    Mini Cheese Fingers, 35
    Muska Boerek, 36
    Red Bell Pepper Paste, 37
    Red Pepper Spread, 38
    Spinach Stems with Walnuts, 39
    Tomato Sauce, 40
    Yogurt, 41

Appetizers (Continued)
    Yogurt Sauce, 43
    Yogurt Spread/Dip with Garlic,
      Dill, and Walnuts, 44
    Yogurt and White Cheese, 45
Apricot(s)
    Dried Apricot Compote, 234
    Dried Apricots Stuffed with
      Cream, 235
    Turkish Dried Apricot Jam, 227
Artichoke Hearts with Vegetables, 195
Arugula Salad, 63
Auntie Melek's Spinach Boerek, 155

B

Baked Lamb Shanks à la Tandour, 116
Baklava, 232
Beans
    Black-Eyed Pea Salad, 65
    Cranberry Beans Pilaki, 198
    Dried Broad Bean Puree, 199
    Fresh Fava Beans in Olive Oil, 201
    Green Beans with Eggs and
      Garlic, 204
    Green Beans in Olive Oil, 203
    Haricot Beans in Olive Oil, 205
    Noah's Pudding, 242
    Pinto Beans in Olive Oil, 208
Beef
    Eggplant Kebabs From Kazan, 119
    Eggplant Moussaka, 120

265

Index

F

G

H

I

J

K

L

M

N

O

P

Index

Index

273

SEPHARDIC ISRAELI CUISINE:
A MEDITERRANEAN MOSAIC
Sheilah Kaufman

Sephardic, derived from the Hebrew word for Spain, defines the Jews of Spain, Portugal, North Africa and the Middle East. The foods of these Mediterranean countries profoundly influenced the Sephardic Israeli cuisine, which abounds with ingredients such as cinnamon, saffron, orange flower water, tahini paste, artichokes, fava beans, couscous, bulgur, persimmons, peaches, and limes.

Sephardic Israeli Cuisine offers 120 kosher recipes that celebrate the colorful and delicious culinary mosaic it represents. Using typical Sephardic ingredients, it includes favorites like Yogurt Cheese; Crescent Olive Puffs; Harira; Tamar's Yemenite Chicken Soup; Grilled Fish with Chermoula; Moroccan Cholent; and Moroccan Sweet Potato Pie.

264 PAGES · 5½ X 8½ · 0-7818-0926-6 · $24.95HC · (21)

THE ART OF TURKISH COOKING
Neşet Eren

Paperback edition of the 1969 classic.
308 PAGES · 5½ X 8½ · 0-7818-0201-6 · $12.95PB · (162)

TURKISH-ENGLISH/ENGLISH-TURKISH DICTIONARY & PHRASEBOOK
Charles Gates

This language guide offers the traveler or new resident in Turkey an excellent reference for communicating immediately in Turkish while acquiring a basic knowledge of the language. The two-way dictionary and phrasebook provides necessary vocabulary and phrases for both travel and daily-life situations. An extensive and comprehensible grammatical introduction teaches the structure and fundamental rules of the language. More complicated phrases are also given to allow the student the chance to practice the grammar presented. A pronunciation guide as well as practical cultural information on Turkish life and culture are included.

- 2,500 dictionary entries
- Pronunciation guide
- Basic Turkish grammar
- Essential phrases
- Cultural information for travelers
- Ideal for the traveler, student, or new resident

2,500 ENTRIES · 228 PAGES · 3¾ X 7 · 0-7818-0904-5 · $11.95PB · (230)

FROM HIPPOCRENE'S COOKBOOK LIBRARY:

A TASTE OF SYRIA
Virginia Jerro Gerbino and Philip M. Kayal

Because of its Aleppian influences, Syrian cuisine is both sophisticated and particularly healthy with its emphasis on lean lamb and vegetables. While some dishes like *Hummus*, *Shish Kabob*, and *Baklava* are well known to Americans and ubiquitous across the Arab world, the foods of Syria are special in their particular mix of spices and textures.

This new compendium of Syrian cuisine includes a brief cultural and historical review, English and Arabic indices of 114 recipes, a glossary of terms, and a guide to the purchase and preparation of ingredients.

220 PAGES · 6 X 9 · 0-7818-0946-0 · $24.95HC · (394)

IMPERIAL MONGOLIAN COOKING:
RECIPES FROM THE KINGDOMS OF GENGHIS KHAN
Marc Cramer

Imperial Mongolian Cooking is the first book to explore the ancient culinary traditions of Genghis Khan's empire, opening a window onto a fascinating culture and a diverse culinary tradition virtually unknown in the West.

These 120 easy-to-follow recipes encompass a range of dishes—from Appetizers, Soups and Salads to Main Courses (Poultry & Game, Lamb, Beef, Fish & Seafood), Beverages and Desserts. Among them are "Bean and Meatball Soup," "Spicy Steamed Chicken Dumplings," "Turkish Swordfish Kabobs," and "Uzbek Walnut Fritters." The recipes are taken from the four *khanates* (kingdoms) of the empire that include the following modern countries: Mongolia, Chinese-controlled Inner Mongolia, China, Bhutan, Tibet, Azerbaijan, Kyrgyzstan, Tajikistan, Turkmenistan, Uzbekistan, Kazakhstan, Georgia, Armenia, Russia, Poland, Ukraine, Hungary, Burma, Vietnam, Iran, Iraq,

Afghanistan, Syria and Turkey. The author's insightful introduction, a glossary of spices and ingredients, and list of sample menus will assist the home chef in creating meals fit for an emperor!

211 PAGES • 5½ X 8½ • ISBN 0-7818-0827-8 • $24.95HC • (20)

CUISINES OF THE CAUCASUS MOUNTAINS
RECIPES, DRINKS, AND LORE FROM ARMENIA, AZERBAIJAN, GEORGIA, AND RUSSIA
Kay Shaw Nelson

People of the Caucasus Mountains, a region comprising Armenia, Azerbaijan, Georgia and Russia, are noted for a creative and masterful cuisine that cooks evolved over the years by using fragrant herbs and spices and tart flavors such as lemons and sour plums. The 184 authentic recipes featured in *Cuisines of the Caucasus Mountains* offer new ways of cooking with healthful yet delectable ingredients like pomegranates, saffron, rose water, honey, olive oil, yogurt, onions, garlic, fresh and dried fruits, and a variety of nuts. The literary excerpts, legends, and lore sprinkled throughout the book will also enchant the reader-chef on this culinary journey to one of the world's most famous mountain ranges.

288 PAGES • 6 X 9 • 0-7818-0928-2 • $24.95HC • (37)

AFGHAN FOOD & COOKERY
Helen Saberi

This classic source for Afghan cookery is now available in an updated and expanded North American edition! This hearty cuisine includes a tempting variety of offerings: lamb, pasta, chickpeas, rice pilafs, flat breads, kebabs, spinach, okra, lentils, yogurt, pastries and delicious teas, all flavored with delicate spices, are staple ingredients. The author's informative introduction describes traditional Afghan holidays, festivals and celebrations; she also includes a section "The Afghan Kitchen," which provides essentials about cooking utensils, spices, ingredients and methods.

312 PAGES • 5½ X 8¼ • ILLUSTRATIONS • $12.95PB • 0-7818-0807-3 • (510)

Prices subject to change without prior notice. To purchase Hippocrene Books contact your local bookstore, call (718) 454-2366, or write to: HIPPOCRENE BOOKS, 171 Madison Avenue, New York, NY 10016. Please enclose check or money order, adding $5.00 shipping (UPS) for the first book, and $.50 for each additional book.